*The Mission of God and the Witness of the Church*

*Short Studies in Biblical Theology*

Edited by Dane C. Ortlund and Miles V. Van Pelt

*The City of God and the Goal of Creation*, T. Desmond Alexander (2018)

*Covenant and God's Purpose for the World*, Thomas R. Schreiner (2017)

*Divine Blessing and the Fullness of Life in the Presence of God*, William R. Osborne (2020)

*From Chaos to Cosmos: Creation to New Creation*, Sidney Greidanus (2018)

*The Kingdom of God and the Glory of the Cross*, Patrick Schreiner (2018)

*The Lord's Supper as the Sign and Meal of the New Covenant*, Guy Prentiss Waters (2019)

*Marriage and the Mystery of the Gospel*, Ray Ortlund (2016)

*The Mission of God and the Witness of the Church*, Justin A. Schell (2024)

*The New Creation and the Storyline of Scripture*, Frank Thielman (2021)

*Redemptive Reversals and the Ironic Overturning of Human Wisdom*, G. K. Beale (2019)

*Resurrection Hope and the Death of Death*, Mitchell L. Chase (2022)

*The Royal Priesthood and the Glory of God*, David S. Schrock (2022)

*The Sabbath as Rest and Hope for the People of God*, Guy Prentiss Waters (2022)

*Sanctification as Set Apart and Growing in Christ*, Marny Köstenberger (2023)

*The Serpent and the Serpent Slayer*, Andrew David Naselli (2020)

*The Son of God and the New Creation*, Graeme Goldsworthy (2015)

*Work and Our Labor in the Lord*, James M. Hamilton Jr. (2017)

"The theme of missions is a key to understanding the Bible. Justin Schell enables us to see this afresh in this book. This is not just a rehashing of previous books on missions, and it is certainly more than an academic book. It is a God-centered call to the church to see the vital place that its Christ-representing witness has in the mission of God. It brings us a message we all need to hear!"

**Conrad Mbewe,** Pastor, Kabwata Baptist Church, Lusaka, Zambia; Founding Chancellor, African Christian University

"Justin Schell provides an excellent overview of mission through the storyline of Scripture. His work reminds us of our identity as a community of witnesses to the work of God in the gospel and gives us a better glimpse of the God whose self-revelation is oriented toward restoring a relationship with his image bearers."

**Trevin Wax,** Vice President of Research and Resource Development, North American Mission Board; Visiting Professor, Cedarville University; author, *The Thrill of Orthodoxy*; *Rethink Your Self*; and *This Is Our Time*

"I am excited to recommend this book. Today there are roughly seven thousand people groups on the planet with little to no access to the gospel. That's more than three billion people. Justin Schell helps the church see the glorious God of mission, his gracious purposes in the world, and our role in that larger work. The reader gets to watch God's mission unfold from the garden of Eden to the new Jerusalem. It's a breathtaking story, and it's our story. We are his witnesses. This book is a wonderful addition to an excellent series."

**Michael Oh,** CEO, Lausanne Movement

"From Genesis to Revelation, Justin Schell shows us God's relentless pursuit of a bride for his Son. This book will do more than shape your view of mission or of Scripture. It will refresh and refocus your view of our great missionary God."

**Glen Scrivener,** evangelist; author, *The Air We Breathe* and *How to See Life: A Guide in 321*; coauthor, *Come and See: A History and Theology of Mission*

"This is a thoroughly readable and well-informed account of God's mission in the world, in which we, as disciples of Christ, are privileged to share. Justin Schell carefully follows the redemptive-historical approach of this series, from the garden to the garden city. Beginning with God's missional activity in creation and its continuation, despite Adam's failure, we see God's purposes unfold through Abraham and the nation of Israel, culminating in the coming of Jesus, God's incarnate missioner, who empowers his people to proclaim repentance and the forgiveness of sins to all people. A feast of biblical insights to enrich our understanding and equip us to glorify God and enjoy him forever."

**Glenn N. Davies,** former Archbishop of Sydney

"Justin Schell carefully traces the theme of mission along the narrative arc of Scripture from Genesis to Revelation. Theologically rich and insightful, this engaging book invites the reader into the drama of Scripture as God reveals, redeems, and restores his creation. Emphasis on communion with the triune God as the aim of mission displays the coherence of the biblical narrative and rightly calls attention to the relational dimension of the *missio Dei*. Refreshing, like the wind of the Spirit, Schell's book draws the contemporary church into the central theme of Scripture and the vital witness of the church."

**Carol Kaminski,** Senior Professor of Old Testament, Gordon-Conwell Theological Seminary

"God made us for communion with himself, so we should care about his mission in the world. In *The Mission of God and the Witness of the Church*, Justin Schell helps us see how God's mission emerges from the story that Scripture tells. Through God's power in judgment and salvation, God is displaying his glory in the world he loves. Schell guides us through the panorama of Scripture as he takes us from Eden to the church's Great Commission. We bear witness to the redemptive work of the triune God, and we long for the consummation of his mission."

**Mitchell L. Chase,** Associate Professor of Biblical Studies, The Southern Baptist Theological Seminary; Preaching Pastor, Kosmosdale Baptist Church, Louisville, Kentucky

# The Mission of God and the Witness of the Church

Justin A. Schell

WHEATON, ILLINOIS

*The Mission of God and the Witness of the Church*

© 2024 by Justin A. Schell

Published by Crossway
              1300 Crescent Street
              Wheaton, Illinois 60187

Cover design: Jordan Singer

First printing 2024

Printed in the United States of America

Trade paperback ISBN: 978-1-4335-8158-8
ePub ISBN: 978-1-4335-8161-8
PDF ISBN: 978-1-4335-8159-5

---

**Library of Congress Cataloging-in-Publication Data**

Names: Schell, Justin A., 1980– author.
Title: The mission of God and the witness of the church / Justin A. Schell.
Description: Wheaton, Illinois : Crossway, 2024. | Series: Short studies in biblical theology | Includes bibliographical references and index.
Identifiers: LCCN 2023032986 (print) | LCCN 2023032987 (ebook) | ISBN 9781433581588 (trade paperback) | ISBN 9781433581595 (pdf) | ISBN 9781433581618 (epub)
Subjects: LCSH: Mission of the Church—Biblical teaching. | Redemption—Biblical teaching.
Classification: LCC BS2545.M54 S34 2024 (print) | LCC BS2545.M54 (ebook) | DDC 266—dc23/ eng/20240126
LC record available at https://lccn.loc.gov/2023032986
LC ebook record available at https://lccn.loc.gov/2023032987

---

Crossway is a publishing ministry of Good News Publishers.

| BP | | 33 | 32 | 31 | 30 | 29 | 28 | 27 | 26 | 25 | 24 |
|----|----|----|----|----|----|----|----|----|----|----|----|
| 15 | 14 | 13 | 12 | 11 | 10 | 9 | 8 | 7 | 6 | 5 | 4 | 3 | 2 | 1 |

*To*
*the mission mobilizers*
*who remind us that the harvest is plentiful*
*but the laborers are few*

# Contents

# Series Preface

Most of us tend to approach the Bible early on in our Christian lives as a vast, cavernous, and largely impenetrable book. We read the text piecemeal, finding golden nuggets of inspiration here and there, but remain unable to plug any given text meaningfully into the overarching storyline. Yet one of the great advances in evangelical biblical scholarship over the past few generations has been the recovery of biblical theology—that is, a renewed appreciation for the Bible as a theologically unified, historically rooted, progressively unfolding, and ultimately Christ-centered narrative of God's covenantal work in our world to redeem sinful humanity.

This renaissance of biblical theology is a blessing, yet little of it has been made available to the general Christian population. The purpose of Short Studies in Biblical Theology is to connect the resurgence of biblical theology at the academic level with everyday believers. Each volume is written by a capable scholar or churchman who is consciously writing in a way that requires no prerequisite theological training of the reader. Instead, any thoughtful Christian disciple can track with and benefit from these books.

Each volume in this series takes a whole-Bible theme and traces it through Scripture. In this way readers not only learn about a given theme but also are given a model for how to read the Bible as a coherent whole.

We have launched this series because we love the Bible, we love the church, and we long for the renewal of biblical theology in the academy to enliven the hearts and minds of Christ's disciples all around the world. As editors, we have found few discoveries more thrilling in life than that of seeing the whole Bible as a unified story of God's gracious acts of redemption, and indeed of seeing the whole Bible as ultimately about Jesus, as he himself testified (Luke 24:27; John 5:39).

The ultimate goal of Short Studies in Biblical Theology is to magnify the Savior and to build up his church—magnifying the Savior through showing how the whole Bible points to him and his gracious rescue of helpless sinners; and building up the church by strengthening believers in their grasp of these life-giving truths.

Dane C. Ortlund and Miles V. Van Pelt

# Abbreviations

Introduction

# The Mission of God

There is a renaissance of scholarship and teaching on the mission of God today. Popular authors and speakers are attempting to help Christians live *on mission*. Mission agencies and church planting networks are training new gospel ministers to start *missional* churches. Missiologists and biblical scholars are exploring *missional readings* of the Bible along with the concept of the *missio Dei*—that is, the mission of God.

Despite all the discussion of mission, a cloud of confusion has descended on the church and academy about what exactly the mission of God is and what the church's role is in it. This stems in part from the fact that *mission* is a slippery word. It has become a catchall word for Christian activity of any kind. When an important word like *mission* becomes so elastic that its meaning is cloudy, significant questions arise.

One such question is, What is the relationship of proclamation ministries such as evangelism, discipleship, and church planting to mercy ministries and efforts to serve the poor, the orphan, and the widow? Even more complex is the question of whether God's mission is just about redeeming mankind or perhaps something larger, even as large as restoring the entire cosmos. This confusion demands that we go back to the Scriptures for answers.

## Defining *Mission*

The English word *mission* is not much used in the Bible.[1] That should not, however, lead us to think that the concept and practice of mission are absent in Scripture.

For our study, I will use the following definition for the mission of God: *God's revelatory work intended to establish a divine-human communion within creation.* Or, as the apostle John puts it in perhaps the most well-known and shared verse in the Bible, "God so loved the world, that he gave his only Son, that whoever believes in him should not perish but have eternal life" (John 3:16). God reveals himself in sending his Son, the Savior, in time and space (i.e., creation), so that mankind might have eternal life, which John defines as knowing God (John 17:3). All of this radiates from God's love for the world. Let's look more closely at the three key terms in our definition: *revelatory work, divine-human communion, within creation.*

### REVELATORY WORK

First, notice that God's mission includes an activity: *God's revelatory work.* Mission is first and foremost something in which God engages: it is from God, through God, and for God. He—not society, government, or even the church—is the primary definer and actor in the *missio Dei.* Before humanity is ever invited into mission, God is at work, revealing himself in revelatory word and saving deed.

You may wonder whether the word *revelation* adequately explains all that God does in creation and redemption. That may be because

---

1. It appears only four times in the English Standard Version, for instance.

we have too low a view of divine revelation. When God speaks, the cosmos is born (Gen. 1). The good news proclaimed is "the power of God for salvation" (Rom. 1:16), and faith comes by hearing (Rom. 10:17) the word of Christ. When we behold the glory of God in the face of Jesus, we are changed from glory to glory (2 Cor. 3:18; 4:4–6). Truly, all that God says and does can be summed up in the word *revelation*—so much so that Jesus declares that his very glory is revealed in his death on the cross (John 12:23–25). God's revelation, in fact, creates and redeems.

This revelatory aspect of God's mission is often connected in mission studies with the Greek verb *apostellō*, which means "send." An apostle (noun: *apostolos*) was literally a "sent one." The Latin verb *mittere* corresponds to *apostellō*. The noun form is *missio*, from which we get our English word *mission*. *Apostellō* captures the idea of *sending* on mission. English speakers might talk about sending an ambassador on a diplomatic mission. For our purposes, throughout Scripture we will see God actively revealing himself through sending. He sends the Son to create and redeem the world by the Spirit, whom he likewise sends. He sends his people, from our first parents to the prophets to the apostle Paul, into the world, as witnesses to his revelation. Each sending is meant to reveal who God is and what he is like. This naturally begs the question, Why is it so important for God to reveal himself?

## Divine-Human Communion

If revelation is the activity of mission, *communion* is the aim of mission, specifically a loving communion between humanity and the living God. This is mission's goal. Perhaps a second Greek word, a noun, will help us understand this aspect of God's mission: *telos*. *Telos* means the desired end. *Telos* tells us why something is done, why it is important, or what we want to achieve. When coupled with what we have already seen, this helps us recognize that all sending (*apostellō*) has a purpose (*telos*). A king sends an ambassador for a reason. A humanitarian mission seeks certain outcomes. This is true, likewise, when God sends.

God reveals himself for communion both in the work of creation and in redemption. At creation, before the fall, the Spirit hovers over the waters to breathe life into the world, and the Word of God speaks everything into existence. Why? The triune God intends to bring humanity into communion with him as children and co-regents. This is also the aim of God's mission in redemption. The cross of Christ is ground zero of a new creation where restored fellowship is made possible as the Spirit of God breathes new life into humanity.

This relational goal of mission is critical to remember. The sending dimension of mission is often the sole focus of missional readings of Scripture. As a result, what is highlighted is simply the church's activities in the world. We truncate God's mission, however, if we neglect the relational heart that undergirds God's sending. This results in two problems.

First, an overly weighted focus on the sending dimension of mission explains why some sections of the Old Testament appear not to apply to God's mission. We clearly see the sending activity in the book of Jonah as missional but fail to see how the Song of Solomon or Hosea, declaring God's plan for communion with humanity, fits into the *missio Dei*. The relational dimension of God's mission helps us make more sense of genres like wisdom and poetry in our biblical theologies of mission.

Second, when we neglect the relational dimension, we don't know what to do with the church beyond involvement in missional activities. But, if God's very aim in his mission is to establish divine-human communion, then the church cannot be reduced to a sending agency.

Some twentieth-century scholars contended that the church has no special role in God's mission; instead, God may fulfill his mission through government and popular uprising more than through the church. Even evangelical scholars have made statements like "it is not so much the case that God has a mission for his church in the world, but that God has a church for his mission in the world. Mission was not made for the church; the church was made for mission."[2] In this way of thinking, the church exists for mission, not the other way around. I will argue the opposite. The revelatory activity of God (and those he sends) is to create and redeem a people for communion.

## WITHIN CREATION

The final part of our definition alerts us to the fact that there is a *setting* for mission. Nonhuman creation has a role in the mission of God. Whether in the garden (Gen. 1–3) or the garden city (Rev. 21–22), the Lord has never intended a bodiless, noncontextual existence for humanity. The cosmos was God's idea; it was to be where his mission would unfold. It has served as the stage on which the great drama of creation, fall, exile, and restoration take place. In eternity future, the new creation will be the everlasting dwelling place of the Lamb and his bride.

The cosmos, whether Edenic, fallen, or renewed, is not the ultimate end of the mission of God; nevertheless, it is the context. Scott Hafemann unpacks this order of relationship when he writes, "Mankind is not created to provide for the world; the world is created to provide for mankind."[3] The creation is good, it is from God, and it exists to host God's designed communion with humanity.

---

2. Christopher J. H. Wright, *The Mission of God: Unlocking the Bible's Grand Narrative* (Downers Grove, IL: InterVarsity Press, 2007), 62.

3. Scott Hafemann, *The God of Promise and the Life of Faith: Understanding the Heart of the Bible* (Wheaton, IL: Crossway, 2001), 28. We will see in chap. 2 that this does not grant us the right to abuse creation. Thus Hafemann continues, "Created in the King's image as his vassals or

So the *missio Dei* has an activity, a purpose, and a context: revelation for communion in creation. These three key terms and their amplifications will become clearer as we move through the narrative of Scripture. If what I have said is correct, we should see this theme naturally emerge from the text as early as the creation narrative (Gen. 1–2), carry right on through into the new creation (Rev. 21–22), and appear everywhere in between.

One facet to our theme that we should prepare for at the outset is that early in the Scriptures we encounter an enemy to God, a being opposed to God's mission. In fact, we encounter three enemies: Satan, sin, and death. While God's mission as I have defined it existed before the fall, much of the narrative focuses on the post-fall restoration necessary to reestablish (and surpass) what has been lost. So the relational purpose remains the same despite the need for new revelatory action on the part of God in the world.

## The Mission of the Church

We have begun to unpack the *missio Dei*, the mission of God. Here I want to take just a moment to ask, what is the role of God's people in his mission? The answer, in short, is that we are his witnesses. God accomplishes his mission, and his people bear witness to what he has done. This may seem to belittle the role of humanity in the mission of God, but perhaps that is because we misunderstand what is meant by *witness*. Much like the word *revelation*, *witness* in the biblical sense points to an awesome reality.

It is through the witness of God's people that the invisible God becomes knowable. Of course, God is most clearly revealed in the incarnation of his Son and in the testimony of Scripture. Our part in the drama is to witness to that revelation in word and deed. We are

---

servants, we thus reflect his character and manifest his glory when we exercise dominion over all he has provided for us with the God-given wisdom and care that characterize God himself" (29).

called to speak lines that will reveal the great author of the universe and the redemption he has wrought. Similarly, we are called to act out our part in a way that reveals his heart and intentions.

How our words and actions work together has been the source of much debate in mission studies. Space limits our ability to fully explore the key positions, but let me speak into the debate briefly. How ought Christians to think of these things? Consider this: Humanity contributed nothing to the work of creation. Just so, God's people supply not one iota to the work of redemption. He has done all. We are his witnesses. We cannot save, but we witness to his saving work. We do not bring the kingdom, but we pray for it, witness to its inauguration, and wait for its full consummation. Do our good works play a role in this? Certainly. We let our good deeds shine so that our neighbors give glory to God (Matt. 5:16).

Our words and deeds reveal truths about God, but in differing ways. When we speak of the doctrine of revelation, we often differentiate between general revelation and special revelation. General revelation includes the ideas, attributes, and concepts about ultimate reality and God that anyone may discern simply by what has been created. For instance, Romans 1:19–20 says: "What can be known about God is plain to them, because God has shown it to them. For his invisible attributes, namely, his eternal power and divine nature, have been clearly perceived, ever since the creation of the world, in the things that have been made. So they are without excuse." Anyone, believer or unbeliever, can see the truth of a powerful Creator if he or she looks at creation without suppressing that truth. This kind of revelation is clear to humanity *in general*.

Special revelation, however, describes the unique revelation God has given us in the gospel and written in Scripture. No amount of general revelation can save a sinner. No one can reason his way from creation to the cross. No, God had to intervene for humanity by the substitutionary life, death, and resurrection of Jesus and communicate it *specially*, so that people might be saved.

In the mission of the church, the proclamation of the gospel saves sinners. Proclamation is the heralding of God's special revelation. Good deeds, in contrast, serve like general revelation. When Christians live lives of love and righteousness, the watching world sees something of God, perhaps his kindness, generosity, provision, or love. But what they learn of God is only a generic, a general revelation. This alone cannot save. No, proclaiming the gospel—the revelation about what God has done through Jesus—is indispensable to our mission. Because of this, in the church's witnessing mission we prioritize proclamation even as we recognize the call to live lives that holistically reflect the truths we believe.

To summarize, God's mission is to reveal himself to humanity throughout the world in order to draw women and men into communion with himself. The role of God's people in this mission is to witness to the revelation of God in word and deed, with priority placed on witnessing to those things revealed by God for salvation, found only in his word.

## The Approach I Am Taking

"Missional" readings of Scripture are multiplying. What is meant by the phrase differs, sometimes wildly, from study to study.[4] While we do not have space for a survey of the missional hermeneutic movement,[5] it is important to share the presuppositions with which I am working and say a few words about how that may differ from others.

---

4. George R. Hunsberger, "Mapping the Missional Hermeneutics Conversation," in *Reading the Bible Missionally*, ed. Michael Goheen (Grand Rapids, MI: Eerdmans, 2016), 45–67.

5. Michael W. Goheen, "A History and Introduction to a Missional Reading of the Bible," in Goheen, *Reading the Bible Missionally*, 3–27.

The approach I am taking may be characterized as an evangelical and redemptive-historical reading: we read the Scriptures as the inspired, inerrant word of God, unfolding a single narrative centered on God's redemptive work in Christ. In doing so, we are following the example of Christ and the apostles (e.g., Luke 24:44–48; Acts 28:23).

The commitment to tracing our theme of the mission of God along the narrative arc of Scripture will help us discern the right emphasis. Another way to say this is that it guards us against turning minor ideas into major issues. This is especially important with a theme like mission, which has a tendency toward atomistic and moralistic readings of Scripture. As the Pharisees made the tithe of dill and cumin more important than the weightier matters of the law, mission studies can sometimes isolate individual commands and then read the rest of Scripture through that lens. Instead, we need to see the big picture of what God is after in the world and allow that to set the agenda.

Seeing God's mission emerge from the biblical narrative also helps guard against reading personal or cultural ideas and agendas into the text. Again, while this may not be a major concern with a theme such as covenant, it can be a strong temptation for the theme of mission; for with mission we often come to Scripture desiring to articulate a biblical foundation for the particular vision or methodology of our organization or institution. And as mission is a global enterprise, undertaken in a dazzling array of nations and ethnicities, we must be extra careful to allow Scripture to be the lens through which we view and judge culture, and not vice versa.

Finally, we are further guarded against these sorts of missteps by reading Scripture intertextually. Later Scripture often sheds light on earlier Scripture, helping us to see with greater clarity. The Old Testament will also inform the New, providing the necessary foundational information on which New Testament authors were building. We therefore read backward and forward. We read Paul to better understand Genesis, but we also read Isaiah to better understand Luke. In this way, we have the clearest vista from which to view the single, unified, unfolding narrative of Scripture that starts in the garden and ends in the garden city, always climaxing in Christ.

To summarize, redemptive history is the mountain range along which the trail of God's mission runs. Is this approach missional? If missional means a way of describing God's purpose and sending in his mission, then I would argue yes. It is a reading that pays attention, first, to God's *telos* as it is expounded throughout the Bible and, then, his sending/work to fulfill that goal.

So we do not read mission into the text. No, we observe what God does and says through the narrative of Scripture so that we see his mission emerging organically from the pages of the Old and New Testaments. When we do this, we will discover a theology of mission with texture and depth, not simply a to-do list or a justification for the missional activity *du jour*.

## The Structure of This Book

It has been said that the whole Bible is about God's mission.[6] In one sense that is true, for the Lord reveals himself and his will to us on every page of Scripture. In another sense, key passages serve as markers along the way that are intended to help us understand the mission of God more explicitly. These key missional passages, intriguingly, overlap with the great sweep of redemptive history running through Scripture (often summed up in the outline of creation, fall, exile, redemption). We will focus on such passages, even while situating them into their surrounding contexts and into the wider narrative.

---

6. Wright, *Mission of God*, 22. See also Richard Bauckham, "Mission as Hermeneutic for Scriptural Interpretation," in Goheen, *Reading the Bible Missionally*, 28.

As we proceed in this manner, we will see our theme develop. More specifically, chapter 1 will introduce us to the *God of mission*. Biblical theologians are increasingly aware of the need to clarify who the God of Scripture is before launching into a thematic study from Genesis to Revelation.[7] Further, we want to explore the purpose behind God's own sending, particularly, the Father's sending the Son in the power of the Spirit in creation and redemption. Our understanding of mission must begin with God—who he is and what his purposes are. John's Gospel, so committed to revealing the Father through the sent Son, will serve as our guide.

Building on chapter 1, the second chapter will then explore how the creation narrative further illuminates the *purpose of mission* I have discussed above—namely, the gathering of men and women into fellowship with God in the newly formed world. In chapter 3, while exploring the patriarchs of Israel, we will see God reveal his *means for mission*, that his purposes will be accomplished by a person, one through whom salvation will come—Abraham's promised seed. Then chapter 4 will reveal, through the picture of the exodus, how the Lord accomplishes his mission. That picture or prototype of salvation will be employed by the rest of Scripture to point to the ultimate rescue to be accomplished by the long-awaited Messiah.

As we will see, these first four chapters give us all we need to understand the mission of God. We will know at that point the God of mission, the purpose of mission, the one through whom the mission will be carried out, and how the mission will be accomplished. These ideas will be further developed in later Scripture; nevertheless, they are clear and meant to be understood very early on in the Pentateuch.

---

7. In fact, Ben Witherington, *Biblical Theology: The Convergence of the Canon* (Cambridge: Cambridge University Press, 2019) spends the first section (112 pp.) exploring the character of God through all of Scripture before returning to Genesis to unpack the Bible's narrative.

Chapter 5, then, will explore how the life of Israel was meant to be one of participation in and witness to God's mission. Unfortunately, we are going to see that, because of the unconverted nature of the majority of the people, the very blessings that were intended to draw more and more men and women into relationship with the God of Israel—the law, the kingdom, and the temple—were going to be co-opted and employed primarily for Israel's own desires. But we will see how, despite Israel's failure, the missional message of the prophets to a people in exile was a repetition and escalation of those truths explored in our first four chapters.

We will then spend two chapters seeing the mission *fulfilled* in Christ and *witnessed to* by the church (chaps. 6–7). Finally, we will conclude by exploring the Epistles and the book of Revelation, marveling at the *consummation* of God's mission.

## Mission Critical

This introduction began by recognizing the abundance of mission teaching and scholarship of late. This abundance is due to the fact that the mission of God is the fulfillment of his purposes in the world. Mission needs to be talked about, studied, and written about. It is critically important. And because of that, we must take extra pains to speak faithfully and clearly about it. Therefore, let us ask the Lord to bless us as we go to his word now so that we might work as master builders, using gold, silver, and precious stones (1 Cor. 3:10–15). And may the Lord be glorified in it all.

# 1

# The God of Mission

In this opening chapter, we want to zero in on the aim of God's mission. Why did he create the world? What is his plan for humanity? Why send Jesus? We must start with these foundational questions before exploring how God accomplishes his mission and what role the church may have in it. Doing so, as I have suggested in the introduction, will be a safeguard for us, ensuring that our theology of mission has God as its foundation. And to do this, let us turn to the Gospel of John.

## The Revelation of God

John's Gospel helps us understand God's mission because he is writing it in order to advance that mission. John says he has "written so that you may believe that Jesus is the Christ, the Son of God, and that by believing you may have life in his name" (20:31). John is writing so that men and women would be drawn into relationship with God. How does John go about that evangelistic work? By revealing the character, the very glory, of God.[1] For John, revelation is the only thing that makes communion possible.

John's prologue prepares the reader to see how God's revelation opens the door for divine-human communion (1:1–18). Jesus is the Word, the Logos, of God (1:1), the one who will help us understand (the logic of) God. The very God who "in the beginning . . . created the heavens and the earth" (Gen. 1:1) is now being revealed by the one who was "in the beginning with God" (John 1:2). Jesus is God and was with God, and he is now revealing the glory of God to the world in his incarnation.

In this way, Jesus is the true light coming to help humanity see God (John 1:4–5, 9). We read that the Word took on flesh in such a way that men could "see his glory" (1:14). It is likely that John expected his readers to know the book of Exodus, for this enfleshed one came and "tabernacled among us" as the one who is "full of grace and truth" (1:14). Indeed, Jesus is "the LORD, the LORD, a God merciful and gracious, slow to anger, and abounding in *steadfast love and faithfulness*" (Ex. 34:6).

Jesus's mission, according to John's prologue, is to reveal God the Father. John 1:18 seems to imply that humanity needs the incarnation, not only to make possible the sacrifice of the Lamb of God but more fundamentally because humanity needs to see the Father: "No one has ever seen God; the only God, who is at the Father's side, he has made him known." How can humanity come to the invisible God? In the Old Testament, the Lord appeared in fire in the bush and at night, in smoke behind the veil, and in lightning on the mountain. He may even have taken on angelic or human form as the angel of the Lord (e.g., Gen. 18, Judg. 13), but he was always veiled. But now the Son has

---

1. So D. A. Carson, *The Gospel according to John*, PNTC (Grand Rapids, MI: Eerdmans, 1991), 90–95, who argues that John's Gospel is an evangelistic document aimed at Jews, calling them to respond to "God's gracious self-disclosure in Jesus" (93).

revealed the Father. "He is the image of the invisible God" (Col. 1:15), his "exact imprint" (Heb. 1:3). In Christ, the glory of God is stamped onto humanity, the Father engraved in the person of his Son for all to read; or as D. A. Carson says, "Jesus is the exegesis of God."[2]

Not only in John's prologue but throughout his ministry, Jesus is disclosing God to mankind. He does this through his *teaching and ministry*. He says that he is speaking the Father's words and wielding the Father's authority (John 7:17–18; 8:28; 12:49–50; 14:10). He reveals the Father through his works. "I can do nothing on my own," says Jesus (John 5:30). His signs reveal the glory of God (2:11; 11:4, 40). With every action Jesus is simply doing what he sees the Father doing (5:19).

He also discloses the Father through his *person*. Christ's "I am" statements in John's Gospel reveal that he is the one who provided food in the wilderness (6:22–59), light for the world (8:12–20; 9:5; 12:46), the God of Abraham (8:58), the way to God (10:7, 9; 14:6), the shepherd of God's people (10:11, 14), the Son of God (10:36), the life-giving God (11:25), the sustainer (15:1–5). He is elsewhere revealed to be the true sacrifice for the sins of the world (1:29), the giver of the water of life (4:7–11; 7:37–39), the suffering servant of Isaiah 53, and the high and lifted-up Lord of Isaiah 6 (John 12:38–41). Each title and metaphor corresponds to the Yahweh we see in the Old Testament.

Perhaps nowhere is the glory of God more clearly displayed than in Jesus's journey to the cross. In his sacrificial death—in falling to the earth and dying like a grain of wheat—Jesus is the revelation of the glory of God (John 12:23–24). While certainly Christ could have intended his resurrection, ascension, and glorification

---

2. Carson, *John*, 135. Exegesis is the approach to biblical studies that seeks the truth of Scripture from within the text, with meaning shining out of its pages, as opposed to an approach that reads our own meaning into it.

in heaven to be included in the statement "the hour has come for the Son of Man to be glorified," the immediate context suggests that his atoning death is central, as does the parallel of John 13:31–32. Of course, these glories do not need to compete. Richard Bauckham argues that they complement each other. The cross, he writes, is "the *climax* of the revelation of God's glory in the flesh." Nevertheless, he says, "it is the degradation and the death, in the light of the resurrection, that constitute the ultimate manifestation of God's glory to the world."[3] And what will be the twofold effect of this victorious sacrifice? First, "the judgment of this world" in which "the ruler of this world [will] be cast out" (John 12:31). And, second, salvation for mankind: "And I, when I am lifted up from the earth, will draw all people to myself" (12:32).

We would have to repeat John's entire Gospel to chronicle all that it reveals about God. In short, John's Gospel reveals Jesus, for to know Jesus is to know the Father. To see Jesus is to see the Father. As Andreas Köstenberger has argued: "Revelation is the overarching category for John in describing the work of the Son."[4] And the design of this divine revelation is that we might believe and be saved and so experience genuine communion with God.

## Communion with God

In Jesus's high priestly prayer (John 17), situated at the end of the intimate Upper Room Discourse, we overhear a conversation (if only one side of it) between God the Father and God the Son. In this prayer, Christ carries us to the very heart of the Father, where we are exposed to some of the clearest truths about who God is, what he is after, and what that means for humanity.

---

3. Richard Bauckham, *Gospel of Glory: Major Themes in Johannine Theology* (Grand Rapids, MI: Baker Academic, 2015), 60–61 (emphasis added).

4. Andreas Köstenberger, *A Theology of John's Gospel and Letters: The Word, the Christ, the Son of God* (Grand Rapids, MI: Zondervan, 2009), 178.

## Eternal Love and Glory

In John 17:5, Jesus prays, "And now, Father, glorify me in your own presence with the glory that I had with you before the world existed." Before there was a cosmos, before there was a world to care for and rule, God the Father and God the Son were sharing glory with one another. In John 17:24, Jesus prays further, "You loved me before the foundation of the world." Before creation was founded, God the Father was loving his Son. The Upper Room Discourse, and especially this prayer, reveals God the Father, God the Son, and God the Spirit eternally existing in a happy communion of mutual *love* and *glory*.

## United in Love and Glory

Jesus's prayer in John 17, however, not only tells us about the nature of God; it also tells us about the plans of God for humanity. We read here of God's desire for not only those in the upper room but all who would believe in Jesus through the witness of the disciples (v. 20). In short, God's plan for humanity is union: that we would be one with Father, Son, and Spirit in their communion of love and glory.

Jesus prays, "The glory that you have given me I have given to them, that they may be one even as we are one" (v. 22). The very glory that has been eternally shared within the Godhead is now being shared by Christ with his people. Jesus summarizes his hope for such a stunning union when he prays in the next verse, "I in them and you in me, that they may become perfectly one, so that the world may know that you sent me and loved them even as you loved me" (v. 23). Notice that final phrase. Not only are men and women now shareholders in the eternal glory of God, but they are also recipients of the eternal love between Father, Son, and Spirit. The Father loves his people "even as" he loves his eternal Son. So much will we share the love of God that we will love Jesus with the very love of the Father (v. 26), and he will love us in the same way (John 15:9).

The Greek word translated "even as" is *kathōs*.[5] John uses it repeatedly in his Gospel to link something that is true about Jesus to those who are his followers. Sometimes the emphasis is on how Jesus brings us into an experience, a relational reality, with the Father that he already has. Sometimes it is on how he mediates to us his own experience or an analogous experience with the Father. Here are just three examples:

- "*As* the living Father sent me, and I live because of the Father, so whoever feeds on me, he also will live because of me" (6:57).
- "I am the good shepherd. I know my own and my own know me, *just as* the Father knows me and I know the Father; and I lay down my life for the sheep" (10:14–15).
- "Jesus said to them again, 'Peace be with you. *As* the Father has sent me, even so I am sending you'" (20:21).

While scattered throughout the Gospel, *kathōs* is used in the prayer of John 17 an astonishing eight times. Through this rich cluster of comparative statements, Jesus's prayer is meant to show us how what Father and Son have shared for all eternity is now, in some sense, being shared with his people. Remember, this is God's plan *before creation*.

This sharing of glory and love is repeatedly described as oneness by Jesus. Jesus and the Father are one, united in shared love and glory. And we are invited into that oneness to share it with them. Consequentially, this spills over into oneness between believers. Or as Bauckham has argued:

---

5. Though translated "even as" in v. 26, we'll see that it may also be rendered "just as" or simply "as."

The general sense . . . is that from the loving communion between the Father and the Son flows the love with which Jesus loved his disciples, a love that enables them to enjoy an intimate, "in-one-another" relationship with Jesus and his Father, and it is from this overflowing of divine love into the world that the oneness of believers among themselves stems.[6]

What the Godhead has known for eternity, a oneness or in-one-another-ness characterized by shared love and glory, is now through the work of Christ made available to humanity. In being united to Christ in fellowship with the Father by the Spirit, we experience redemption, for eternal life is knowing God (v. 3). That is the Christian hope for mankind.

Notice too the missional impact of this in-one-another-ness. What happens when men and women are swept up into this rich fellowship with the triune God? It has a witnessing effect in the world. In John 17:21–23, Jesus twice says that our oneness with God and with each other testifies to the world that Jesus is the one sent to reveal the Father. Just as this sort of salvation explains the transformative power of the Spirit in the life of a believer, for who can truly share in eternal love and glory and not be changed, it also explains the missional compulsion within true Christianity. For as the love of the Father for the Son cascades into the life of the believer by the power of the Spirit, it cannot help but overflow as well into the world. In both senses, we become like the one to whom we are united.

## What Is God's Mission?

And that brings us to the point of our book. What is the triune God after in the world? He has revealed himself in time and space in order to bring many sons and daughters into his family (John 1:12).

---

6. Bauckham, *Gospel of Glory*, 36.

You were made for communion with the living God, to share in his glory and love. The Scriptures are given to us for this reason (John 5:39–40). Jesus desires that we be with him (John 17:24). He desires that we would know the one true God and have life (John 17:3). However else we may define the mission of God, if we miss this, we miss everything because we will miss God himself.

William Hendriksen summarizes this mission, so clearly articulated in Christ's prayer, when he writes, "The Son is looking forward to the glory of rejoicing in the joy of his saved people, the very people whose salvation he (together with the Father and the Spirit) had planned from eternity, before the world existed."[7]

Let us consider one more verse, John 20:21. What does Jesus mean when he says, "As the Father has sent me, even so I am sending you"? Or asked differently, in what way is our being sent by Jesus similar to the Father's sending of Jesus? We have seen that Jesus was sent to reveal the glory of God (John 1:14) so that people may know God as Father (John 1:12, 18) through Christ's redemptive work (John 3:16–18). Further, we have seen that believing what has been revealed is what saves lost men and women (John 20:31), allowing them to share in the very communion of the Trinity (John 17).

If that is true, then our sent-ness must likewise be revelatory. The cry of desperate humanity is "We must see God." And so the church declares what God has done in Christ. We declare the glory-soaked, bloodstained cross (John 12:23–26) and provide proof that Jesus is from the Father through our love for God and one another (John 17:20–23). In short, we witness to what God has done in Christ so that many more would believe through us (John 17:20).

And as we transition to the creation narrative in the next chapter, we want to keep God at the center of our discussion. For much of

---

7. William Hendriksen, *John*, NTC (Grand Rapids, MI: Baker, 1983), 352.

the history of evangelicalism, discourse on the mission of God has tended toward anthropocentrism—that is, a focus on the needs of humanity. So the lostness of man has been the driving force for mission—or perhaps attempts to understand and engage human culture or to repair evils within society. While these are important conversations within mission, we must not start with man or society—with lostness, sinfulness, or brokenness.

More recently, cosmocentrism, the care and cultivation of creation, has been the focus of much reflection on the mission of God. While we should note the importance of creation in the mission of God, we must remember that God's mission flows from eternity past. The cosmos is a subsequent reality to the love and glory shared within the Godhead. We should not discourage Christians who foster human flourishing of all kinds in this age; on the contrary, we must applaud and support them. We also look forward with delight to the renewal of the cosmos we will experience in the age to come. Nevertheless, we do not give these things the place of God in the mission of God.

When we start with mankind or creation in our reflections on mission, we often forget to include God. But if we begin with God and keep him central to our discussions, asking, "What is God after?" the many needs of humanity, society, and even the cosmos find their rightful place within his plan of redemption. So, now that we have fixed our eyes on the nature and subsequent plan of God, let us look at Genesis 1–3 to see God's mission as it enters time and space.

# 2

# Mission in the Garden

The Bible does not open with a purpose statement or an explanatory introduction. God simply begins his creative work. He creates the heavens and the earth and all that is necessary for this new reality to endure. He does all of this without saying why he is doing it, only that it is "good." But in Genesis 1:26 there is a shift. Here we begin to encounter God's purpose in his creative activity:

> Then God said, "Let us make man in our image, after our likeness. And let them have dominion over the fish of the sea and over the birds of the heavens and over the livestock and over all the earth and over every creeping thing that creeps on the earth."
>
> So God created man in his own image,
> > in the image of God he created him;
> > male and female he created them.
>
> And God blessed them. And God said to them, "Be fruitful and multiply and fill the earth and subdue it, and have

dominion over the fish of the sea and over the birds of the heavens and over every living thing that moves on the earth." (Gen. 1:26–28)

In verse 26, we read of God creating humanity. While there is debate over the significance of the first-person-plural pronouns ("us" and "our") in verse 26, most interpreters agree that we are observing some type of disclosure by God (within himself, to the angels, or perhaps to the earth itself).[1] God's disclosure reveals his purpose. The Lord has one more creature to unveil, but it will differ from what has come before it. Everything he has made is good, but this final member will provide the logic for everything before it; or, as Gerhard von Rad argues: "At the very end of the succession is man. . . . The world is oriented toward man, and in him it has its purest direct relation to God."[2] This final creation will be the culmination of God's creative work. Without this final addition, creation would not make sense. Mankind is, literally, the *telos* of God's creation—the purposeful end toward which everything is progressing.

This declaration of one final creation signals a narrative shift, a shift that will determine whether our definition of God's mission as *revelation for communion in creation* is something imposed on Scripture or, as I will argue, something that is developing organically out of it.

## Revelation through the Image of God

In one sense, God has been revealing himself in Genesis 1:1–25. In those verses we encounter the life-giving Spirit of God (v. 2) and the world-shaping Word of God (v. 3 and elsewhere). Paul tells us

---

1. See a survey of the various positions in Gordon Wenham, *Genesis 1–15*, WBC 1 (Waco, TX: Word, 1987), 27–28. I would argue that this usage reflects the triune nature of God.

2. Gerhard von Rad, *Old Testament Theology: The Theology of Israel's Traditions* (Louisville: Westminster John Knox, 2001), 66.

in Romans 1:20 that the creation reveals the invisible attributes of God. But now God makes man, a creature able to see and receive God's revelation. Not only does man receive God's revelation, but he is meant to reflect it in the world.

God has made mankind *in his image, after his likeness* (Gen. 1:26). What this means precisely is critical for discerning the Lord's purpose in creating humanity. Suggestions for what is meant by the "the image of God" (*imago Dei*) range from walking upright to having free will.[3] We find some direction, however, in the language and context of our passage. The Hebrew word *tselem*, used for image, is employed elsewhere to describe carved images such as idols (1 Sam. 6:5). Almost exclusively in the Old Testament, the image is a physical representation. Similarly, in the surrounding nations, image language is used of statues of Assyrian kings, idols representing or inhabited by deities, and in the case of Egypt, Pharaoh as the image of a god.

In light of this, most scholars conclude that there is a representational aspect to humanity in the image of God, with some even suggesting that the translation would be better rendered as "Let us make man *as* our image."[4] This would mean that man does not have some characteristic that makes him like God (rationality, righteousness, etc.) but instead serves as that which represents and reveals God in creation. Whether one accepts this translation, the idea of representation is clear. And it is strengthened as we look at another, related word.

Man is made in the image of God, after his *likeness*. Likeness can be seen as simply a poetic repetition of image, though it may also clarify that God does not have a physical image. Nevertheless, likeness supports a representational role for humanity. Mankind is

---

3. For a summary of views, see David J. A. Clines, "The Image of God in Man," *Tyndale Bulletin* 19 (1968): 54–61.
4. Clines, "Image of God," 79.

meant to image, to reveal God. We could even say that man, by his very existence, witnesses to God.

The very next line of Genesis 1:26 seems to clarify what the image does, what it is created for. The man and woman, made in the image of God, are to "have dominion" over the rest of creation. Man and woman are created beings, so they are clearly not the sovereign Creator of the universe. That is God. Yet they are not like the rest of creation either, as they are commissioned to exercise the Creator's authority in his world. Perhaps this is on the mind of David in Psalm 8 when he strives to comprehend the high position the Lord has given man in his world. The same God who made the cosmos in all its grandeur also made humans from dust. They are made a little lower than God, making them fit not to replace him but to represent him.

It is interesting to note one difference between scriptural teaching on this topic and that of the surrounding cultures of the ancient Near East. Outside of the biblical narrative, being made in the image of a god is almost always used to describe royalty—an Assyrian king or Egyptian pharaoh. As the image of the deity, they are his vice-regents, ruling on earth in his stead. What is unique, however, about the biblical understanding of the image of God is that it is applied to all people, not just rulers. Serving as vice-regents of the Creator God is a part of what it means to be human, for every person, both men and women.

And as the language of *image* suggests, our rule ought to reflect God's rule. Because the man and woman are under the benevolent care of the sovereign Lord, they must also exercise a benevolent rule over the creation. Theirs is no tyrannical authority over the birds, fish, and animals but a caring stewardship on behalf of God, a stewardship that flows out of a relationship with their Creator.

## Created for Communion

To this point, I have primarily spoken of what the image of God does. Now we want to press into what the image is. Mankind in God's image has a representational purpose, but it also has a relational substance. In the most basic sense, being created in the image of God means that there is some correspondence between man and God. Humans can relate to God *because* they are made in God's image. The animals do not relate to God in such a way. No, the relational ability to commune and co-reign rests with mankind alone.

But there is something deeper to this relationality. Catherine McDowell has argued convincingly that to be made in the image of God reflects kinship, specifically sonship.[5] Just as Seth's sonship is described as being in the likeness and after the image of Adam (Gen. 5:3), so Adam is God's son made in God's image. Luke's Gospel can thus affirm that the first man was "Adam, the son of God" (3:38). This would suggest a contrast in the creation account of Genesis 1. The trees, birds, and animals reproduce offspring "according to their kinds" (vv. 11–12, 21–25), but the language of "kinds" is not used of humanity. McDowell explains:

> The creation of the first human pair is not described as "according to its kind," as might be expected, but as "in the image of God." This juxtaposition of the repeated "according to its/their kind" with "in the image of God" suggests at least two things. First, Genesis 1 draws a sharp distinction between humanity (male and female) and the other created beings; second, just as the plants and animals were created according

---

5. Catherine McDowell, "In the Image of God He Created Them," in *The Image of God in an Image Driven Age: Explorations in Theological Anthropology*, ed. Beth Felker Jones and Timothy W. Barbeau (Downers Grove, IL: InterVarsity Press, 2016), 29–46.

to their own type, humanity was made according to God's kind, metaphorically speaking.[6]

Man and woman are sons of God,[7] and this relational reality undergirds the royal function I have already discussed. It is because Adam is a son, an heir, of God that he is called upon to exercise dominion within his father's creation. The heir has royal responsibilities, but the heir also has a priestly role.

Genesis 2:15 reads, "The LORD God took the man and put him in the garden of Eden to work it and keep it." Scholars have noted that forms of the Hebrew words translated "work" and "keep" are also used (often together) in priestly contexts (Ex. 3:12; Num. 3:7–8; 8:26; 18:5; 28:2). The labor assigned to the first humans was meant to be holy work, much like the later Levitical care for the tabernacle or temple's sacred premises and articles. This means that Adam and Eve's work was of a priestly nature, relating to God on behalf of creation and relating to creation on behalf of God.

This definition of image as sonship corresponds with what we discovered in John's Gospel, that the relationship which the Son has with the Father is shared with humanity through the work of the Spirit. Jesus, "the image of the invisible God, the firstborn of all creation" (Col. 1:15), shares his rights as Son with those who believe (John 1:12; 3:16). So, too, Paul will argue that we are predestined to be conformed to the *image* of Jesus, "the firstborn among many brothers" (Rom. 8:29; see also Col. 1:15). How are we fashioned back into the image of God in Christ? God gives us the "Spirit of adoption as sons" who leads us to call God "Abba! Father!" We are never more like Jesus, never more son-like, than when we are in warm relation-

---

6. McDowell, "In the Image of God," 38.
7. I maintain the language of a male "son" as it reflects the ancient Near Eastern practice of regarding sons as heirs. Nevertheless, both males and females are created as "sons"/heirs of God the Father.

ship with God the Father (Rom. 8:14–17). This adoption as sons was God's will at creation. In fact, he elected us to adoption "before the foundation of the world" (Eph. 1:4–5). In accord with John, Paul declares that sonship was God's design for man from the beginning, and it is now possible by the Spirit for those who are in Christ, the man of heaven (1 Cor. 15:49).

## One Flesh

We must consider one more aspect of relationality between humans and God as we encounter it in the garden of Eden. The creation narrative ends with the marriage of the man and woman: "Therefore a man shall leave his father and his mother and hold fast to his wife, and they shall become one flesh" (Gen. 2:24). There was something "very good" about the male and the female joined in marriage in the mind of God.

Lest we begin to think that human marriage is the ultimate point here, consider Genesis 2:24 as interpreted by Paul in Ephesians 5:25–32:

> Husbands, love your wives, as Christ loved the church and gave himself up for her, that he might sanctify her, having cleansed her by the washing of water with the word, so that he might present the church to himself in splendor. . . . "Therefore a man shall leave his father and mother and hold fast to his wife, and the two shall become one flesh." This mystery is profound, and I am saying that it refers to Christ and the church.

In Ephesians 5:31, Paul quotes Genesis 2:24—the description of marriage given by God at the consummation of the first marriage—and says plainly that the verse is about Jesus and the church. We must wrestle with the ramifications of that statement. Paul is not saying the marriage of man and woman reminded God of his own love. No, when the Lord announces the marriage of the first humans in the garden and before the fall, he is revealing what his own purpose is in creation—namely, an expansion of his family. We are not only sons of the Father but also the bride of Christ.

Therefore, as the capstone to the creation narrative, Genesis 2:24 illustrates that God has created the heavens and the earth so that there might be relationship, something like marital fealty, between God and humanity. The creation account does not hesitate to draw a line of distinction between humanity and the rest of creation. While creation is good and the beautiful handiwork of God, it does not exist for itself. Paul agrees. Creation exists so that humanity might come into union with the triune God.[8]

### In the Garden, to the World

Above, we noted a similarity in the language of working and keeping the garden with that used for the care of the temple. The resemblance between garden and temple goes much deeper than lexical similarities in Genesis 2:15. Gordon Wenham describes several parallels between Eden and the later tabernacle and temple structures of Israel.[9] These similarities include the fact that both Eden and the temple face eastward. The Most Holy Place within the temple is guarded by cherubim, the same heavenly beings who guard the entrance to Eden after the fall. The temple is decorated from floor to ceiling with

---

8. This is similar to Jonathan Edwards, *The "Miscellanies," Entry Nos. a–z, aa–zz, 1–500*, ed. Thomas A. Schafer (New Haven, CT: Yale University Press, 1994), 271–72, where he argues that the marriage between Christ and humanity is the end for which God created the world.

9. Gordon J. Wenham, "Sanctuary Symbolism in the Garden of Eden Story," in *Proceedings of the World Congress of Jewish Studies* (Jerusalem: World Union of Jewish Studies, 1986), 19–25. See also Catherine McDowell, "Human Identity and Purpose Redefined: Gen 1:26–28 and 2:5–25 in Context," *Advances in Ancient, Biblical, and Near Eastern Research* 1, no. 3 (Autumn 2021): 29–44.

garden images, such as lilies, palm trees, gourds, and pomegranates, as well as adorned with precious metals and stones that would have been found in the region of Eden.

Perhaps most important, Eden and the temple are the holy contexts in which God meets with humanity. G. K. Beale writes, "The same Hebrew verbal form (hithpael), *hithallek*, used for God's 'walking back and forth' in the Garden (Gen. 3:8), also describes God's presence in the tabernacle (Lev. 26:12; Deut. 23:14 [15]; 2 Sam. 7:6–7)."[10] The first humans were priests before God, not only serving but also dwelling in the Most Holy Place. They stood relationally between God (cultic worship) and the world (cultivating/having dominion). Said another way, Eden was a place where God tabernacled among us.

But this garden temple where man and God communed was never meant to stay tucked away in the Near East. The Lord blessed mankind and said, "Be fruitful and multiply and fill the earth and subdue it" (Gen. 1:28). This Edenic commission begins in a garden but is global in scope. The earth by God's command is meant to be filled, filled with a humanity who images God and who will lovingly cultivate creation as God's priest-kings. Considering later exhortations, such as the promise that Abram's seed would bless all the peoples (Gen. 12:1–3) and the mandate of Christ to make disciples of all nations (Matt. 28:18–20), we can be confident that this charge to fill the earth was more than simply poetic hyperbole. No, it is early evidence of the global nature of God's mission.

The working and keeping of the garden from the very beginning were meant to spread throughout the entire world until the whole earth was a garden temple in which man and woman would fellowship with the gracious Creator God.[11] *Even before the fall*, we

---

10. G. K. Beale, "Eden, the Temple, and the Church's Mission in the New Creation," *Journal of the Evangelical Theological Society* 48, no. 1 (March 2005): 7.

11. The most extensive argument for this is found in G. K. Beale, *The Temple and the Church's Mission: A Biblical Theology of the Dwelling Place of God*, NSBT 17 (Downers Grove, IL:

see that the mission of God is his revelatory work intended to keep humanity in (or, later, to bring humanity into) loving fellowship with the living God in the world that he made. How did Adam and Eve participate in the *missio Dei*? They represented God as sons, priest-kings reflecting him and his reign in the world. They were his witnesses in all creation.

## The Mission in Peril

While we cannot explore all there is to say about the fall and its ramifications, it is important to see how it serves as a direct challenge to the goal of God's mission in the world. The fall represents a three-part loss to match the three-part mission.

First, *the revelation of God is challenged*. The serpent questions God's word to Adam and Eve, and the first parents believe the lie. As a precursor to the searing indictment by Paul in Romans 1, we learn in Genesis 3 that rejecting God's revelation and engaging in idolatry run in the human family. For although Adam and Eve "knew God, they did not honor him as God or give thanks to him, but they became futile in their thinking, and their foolish hearts were darkened. Claiming to be wise, they became fools, and exchanged the glory of the immortal God" for created things (Rom. 1:21–23). Humanity has rejected the truth.

Second, when God's revelation is rejected, *communion is impossible*. Sin enters the world, man is alienated from God, and Adam and Eve run for cover (Gen. 3:8). Fear replaces fellowship. Concealment, not communion, is their response to God's presence in the garden. In fact, fellowship with God is no longer possible. They are sent east of Eden. To modern ears this may sound like simple geography, but we are being prepared to understand the ultimate

InterVarsity Press, 2004); see esp. 81–122.

consequences of sin. This becomes clearer in Genesis 4, where Cain will be sent "away from the presence of the LORD" (v. 16). Sent away—our theology of hell begins here. East of Eden is preparing us for outer darkness (Matt. 8:12; 22:13; 25:30). Away from God becomes the horrifying "outside" of Revelation 22:14–15, forever cut off from the tree of life. Humanity's reality is eternal death (Gen. 2:17; Eph. 2:1).

Nevertheless, in love God confronts the man and the woman. While there will be pain in childbearing and in working the ground, which is cursed, the Lord speaks a promise of redemption over his now sinful children. More specifically, he promises that their enemy and the consequences of his evil will be destroyed by an offspring of the woman (Gen. 3:15). A descendent of Adam and Eve would one day defeat the serpent Satan (Rev. 12:9), and in so doing, he will bring about renewed communion between God and man.

Third, *humanity is expelled from Eden*. The holy place where God's own presence dwells is no longer accessible to humanity, because of sin. The place where mankind's dominion was meant to originate and spread is now off-limits. Questions now arise over whether humanity, representing the Lord, or the serpent holds dominion over the earth. Though humans continue to bear the image of God, the world is now under the sway of the evil one (1 John 5:19).[12] Humanity needs a way back to God.

Even this exile, however, should be seen as a gracious act on the part of God. This punishment's aim is to thwart mankind, "lest he reach out his hand and take also of the tree of life and eat, and live forever" (Gen. 3:22). The impression given in the passage is that it is possible for mankind to live in a sinful state, alienated from God forever. Instead of permitting this "hell on earth," the Lord sends

---

12. This is not to suggest that the godly no longer serve as God's vice-regents, but instead to point out that their work is not only more difficult but also contested.

Adam and Eve out of the garden, carrying with them the promise of a redemption strong enough to overcome their approaching death.

## Redemptive Mission

Truth is rejected. Humanity's natural state is death. The first couple is sent away from God. They need the way, the truth, and the life.

We noticed already that the seed of Eve is promised to undo the work of the enemy. Stephen Dempster rightly argues that the seed of the woman is the answer to both the problem of lost relationship and the problem of lost dominion; or as he puts it, the seed brings "genealogical and geographical hope."[13] This serpent-crushing seed will not make it through unscathed, however. By the time he is finished, he will have become a curse himself (Gal. 3:13). He will know the abject horror of being God-forsaken (Mark 15:34). Death will open wide its mouth to consume him (Mark 15:45). It will be through his suffering that the enemy will be destroyed and humanity restored (Heb. 9:12–14, 26; 10:10–14).

What we know for certain by the end of Genesis 3 is that the Lord's desire is for humanity to dwell with him as sons, partnering with him in his good, global rule over creation. Despite the fall, the Lord's desire, his purpose, has not changed. The rest of Scripture will unpack more fully the details of his restoration plan.

In the next chapter, as we depart Eden, we are going to find out that God's plan of redemption through the promised Redeemer will center on one family, a family through whom the Lord will work to bless all the families of the earth.

---

13. Stephen G. Dempster, *Dominion and Dynasty: A Biblical Theology of the Hebrew Bible*, NSBT 15 (Downers Grove, IL: InterVarsity Press, 2004), 68–72.

# 3

# Father of All Nations

We leave Eden with hope of redemption, but rescue and renewal do not come quickly. Genesis 3:15 sets the stage for what is to come. Speaking to the serpent, the Lord says,

> I will put enmity between you and the woman,
>> and between your offspring and her offspring;
> he shall bruise your head,
>> and you shall bruise his heel.

In these short lines we discover three realities. First, we see that a redeemer will come, and by his own suffering he will put right all that has gone wrong. Second, we notice that there is an enemy who wants to destroy humanity and, especially, this promised seed. There is enmity, hostility between the enemy and the seed of the woman.

The third thing we notice is that all of humanity is divided now. Every person is either an offspring of Eve or an offspring of Satan. This theme will run from Genesis through the entire canon. Jesus will call those who oppose him children of their "father the devil"

(John 8:44). Paul will call them "sons of disobedience" (Eph. 2:2–3), and John will later call them the "synagogue of Satan" (Rev. 2:9; 3:9). But those who receive the Christ, the seed of Eve, will rightfully be called "children of God" (John 1:12).

Genesis 4–9 traces the development of these two families. The seed of the serpent grows in number and in evil, from Cain's fratricide to the contemporaries of Noah and the flood. The lineage of the woman, through Seth, comprises those who live by faith (Heb. 11:4–7) in the promised deliverer and "call upon the name of the LORD" (Gen. 4:26).

This division within humanity is the reason that Genesis focuses so intently on childbearing. The narrative seems to move from one childbearing emergency to another. All of the genealogies of Genesis exist for the same reason—to track the seed of promise. Genealogies look to the fulfillment of the promise of God that a Savior will come. They are the gospel in family-tree form.[1]

The line of Seth leads us to Noah. Noah, as his name suggests, does bring a kind of rest to the world, but not as we might hope. Whether we understand the beginning of Genesis 6 as describing fallen angels seeking to procreate evil offspring with human women or simply intermarriage between the line of Eve and the "offspring" of the serpent (an oft repeated occurrence in the Old Testament), the narrative suggests that a faithful remnant composed of a single family is all that remains. It is a family led by the man of faith, Noah.

So the world is first cleansed and then renewed by the flood. The promised seed will carry on through Shem (Gen. 9:26). In the promise to Japheth, we catch a glimpse of what will become clearer later in Scripture—namely, that many nations will find their redemption by identifying with the promised seed (Gen. 9:27) in the line of Shem.

---

1. That is why the last genealogies in the Bible are Matthew's and Luke's. The Savior seed has come. Jesus is here. There is no need for more genealogies.

And there remains a calling from God on humanity to "be fruitful and multiply and fill the earth" (Gen. 9:1, 7). The priestly calling to reflect and represent God remains.

Though the relationship between creation and humanity has become even more strained (Gen. 9:2) and sin continues as an ever-present reality in this world (Gen. 8:21), God remains committed to a world filled with men and women in communion with him. In fact, he establishes a covenant with all of creation to make sure that his purposes can move forward despite their sin (Gen. 9:8–11). In the Noahic covenant, the Lord reveals himself as supremely patient, merciful, and utterly committed to the mission.

## The Nations and Babel

Genesis 4–9 is leading up to Abram, but chapters 10 and 11 provide the background to Abram's election and missional calling. In Genesis 10, we encounter the Table of Nations, a list of peoples descended from Noah's three sons, Shem, Ham, and Japheth. In chapter 11, at the Tower of Babel we discover how these descendants become both geographically scattered and culturally distinct. This futile cosmic coup on the plain of Shinar will prepare us for the next major development in the history of redemption. We are told in Genesis 11:1–4:

> Now the whole earth had one language and the same words. And as people migrated from the east, they found a plain in the land of Shinar and settled there. . . . Then they said, "Come, let us build ourselves a city and a tower with its top in the heavens, and let us make a name for ourselves, lest we be dispersed over the face of the whole earth."

In response to God's call to Noah and his descendants to fill the earth, humanity intends to settle in one place. Instead of seeking to image the glory of God throughout all of creation, they intend to make a name for themselves. But the Lord will come and *graciously* defy their empire building by confusing their languages (v. 7).

As the families of the earth attempt to make a name for themselves, the Lord is about to elect one family to bless all the scattered peoples of the earth (Gen. 12:3). As these gathered rebels seek to establish their own name and renown, the Lord is choosing a son of Shem (Heb.: "name"): Abram, to whom the Lord says, "I will . . . make your name great" (Gen. 12:2). Finally, as this rebellious multitude seeks to storm the gate of God (*babel*), God confuses (*balal*) their language so that, ultimately, he might reveal himself on earth. In ignorance and sin, the multitude at Babel wanted glory, blessing, and heaven. They did not yet understand that the living God was already planning to share those things with humanity.

So the Lord scatters humanity over the face of the whole earth. While this dispersal is a judgment, I have argued that it is gloriously gracious. Genesis 11:6 suggests that a single-culture humanity consisting of the seed of Satan and gathered against the living God would exercise near-limitless evil. The merciful God intervenes so that the mission may continue, so that mercy might be granted. Humanity is now divided into what we today call ethnolinguistic peoples. Perhaps in the twenty-first century, we are quick to think of a diversity of cultures and languages as a central piece to the mission of God. This is true because of Babel. God's mission was global from the beginning, even before the fall in the garden. Now, we discover that his mission includes all peoples and languages. This will become clearer as we move forward in the narrative.

## Father Abraham

After the depravity and rebellion of the previous chapters, these next few verses blow like a fresh breeze, bringing hope and bearing away despair. These verses will be quoted and echo throughout the rest of Scripture. The promises of Genesis 12:1–3 lay out God's method for accomplishing his mission, so we will spend the rest of the chapter attempting to understand them more fully.

> Now the LORD said to Abram, "Go from your country and your kindred and your father's house to the land that I will show you. And I will make of you a great nation, and I will bless you and make your name great, so that you will be a blessing. I will bless those who bless you, and him who dishonors you I will curse, and in you all the families of the earth shall be blessed."

## REVELATION FOR COMMUNION

We have no reason to think that Abram knew God before this encounter in Ur. Instead, it is the Lord who initiates. Yahweh speaks to Abram. It will be the Lord who, again and again in the life of Abram, reveals himself in order to continue his plan. And what is revealed here? In short, the promised seed of the woman will, by God's sovereign blessing, come through Abram's lineage and save those who place their faith in that promised seed.

Building on this revelation, the Lord calls Abram to leave house and home because his purpose is to create a new nation, a people for his own possession. Notice that the Lord is not sending Abram to the promised land. Instead, he is *leading* Abram to the land. The Lord is, in the commission to go, creating a people for communion. And the repeated altar building on the part of Abram demonstrates that he is aware of the Lord's presence with him (Gen. 12:7, 8; 13:18). Let's look a little more closely at our passage.

In Genesis 12:1–3 and related promises to Abram/Abraham (e.g., Gen. 15, 17), the Lord is promising blessing for Abram and his soon-to-be family. He will receive land, descendants, and a name. Promise after promise pours over Abram. But these blessings for Abram are headed somewhere.

The blessings for Abram are part of God's plan to get *the* blessing to all the families or nations of the earth.[2] God will bless Abram, and he will be a blessing to all the families of the earth through a promised offspring.[3] And with the curses of Genesis 3 still looming, the theme of blessing through a seed should alert the reader to a reversal of the curses from the garden. However, to understand most clearly what that blessing will be, we must consider Paul's understanding of Genesis 12 in Galatians 3.

## Justification through Faith

In Galatians 3, after having argued against a works-based salvation, Paul is making a positive argument for a grace-based salvation. In short, he argues that anyone who has ever been saved is saved in the same way as Abraham, the father of the faith (v. 7). Quoting Genesis 15:6, Paul argues that Abraham was saved through faith. "Abraham 'believed God, and it was counted to him as righteousness'" (Gal. 3:6).

What is remarkable for our purposes is what Paul says next. In verse 8, Paul explains that the salvation not only of Abraham but of all nations is the point of the promises of Genesis 12:1–3. For he says in verse 8, "And the Scripture, foreseeing that God would justify the Gentiles by faith, preached the gospel beforehand to Abraham, saying, 'In you shall all the nations be blessed.'"

First, notice that for Paul, "in you shall all nations be blessed" is the content of the gospel. As Thomas Schreiner argues, "Paul identi-

---

2. Gen. 18:18; 22:18; and 26:4 will speak of "nations" in place of "families."
3. The promise of blessing becomes more specific as something that comes through Abraham's seed, offspring, or descendant. See Gen. 22:18; 26:4; 28:14.

fies the promise of universal blessing *as the gospel* in Gal 3:8."[4] How is that statement "the gospel"? In many ways it is the repetition of the promise of Genesis 3:15: an offspring of Eve will come to reverse the curse. That's the good news in seed form.

Notice, too, that Gentiles are blessed by this good news *through faith*. They are justified by faith. Faith in what? For the original readers of Genesis, faith in the promised son of Abraham who would redeem humanity from the fall despite a blow from the enemy. For the Galatians, faith in the salvation accomplish by the Christ—dead, buried, risen, and glorified—bringing many sons into Abraham's family through faith (Gal. 3:7, 29).

Consider further this promised offspring. I have hinted at it already, but Paul in Galatians 3:16 is wonderfully explicit: "Now the promises were made to Abraham and to his offspring. It does not say, 'And to offsprings,' referring to many, but referring to one, 'And to your offspring,' who is Christ." It is not completely clear which Genesis text Paul is quoting. The most likely options include 13:15 and 17:8. Because "offspring" or "seed" can be a collective singular, some scholars have accused Paul of allegorical interpretation or, worse, simply twisting the text to his own purpose; however, if we have taken seriously the theme of the Savior seed flowing out of Genesis 3:15, a singular reading is the only one that makes sense.

Finally, what more can be said about this blessing? In short, it is a reverse of the curse. Paul declares that the blessing of Genesis 12, fulfilled in Christ, brings complete repair of the curses of Genesis 3 when he argues, "Christ redeemed us from the curse of the law by becoming a curse for us . . . so that in Christ Jesus the blessing of Abraham might come to the Gentiles" (Gal. 3:13–14). Not only does faith in Christ bring the Gentiles into Abraham's family, but even more

---

4. Thomas R. Schreiner, *Galatians*, ZECNT (Grand Rapids, MI: Zondervan, 2010), 190 (emphasis added).

importantly, it brings them into God's family (Gal. 4:5–7). So we can sum up the heart of the call of Abram in Genesis 12:1–3 in this way: the promise of the coming seed to reverse the curse is announced (revelation) in order that men and women might believe it and be brought into the family of God (communion) from every nation.

Galatians 3 interprets the promises of God to Abram in such a way as to clarify both the person through whom salvation will come (the Messiah, the promised seed of Eve, will now come through Abram's family) and how that salvation will be applied to sinful men and women (reckoned to them, as they are declared righteous through faith). Land, offspring, and name are promised and given *so that* all the families/nations of the earth will be blessed by hearing of and believing in the Redeemer to come and so experience salvation by grace through faith. And Abram knows it (John 8:56).

## WORLDWIDE BLESSING

Abram and his people will be blessed by the Lord in such a way that they grow numerically but also representationally. Yes, they will bear children of their own, but men and women from other families, other clans, will join Abram's family. They will be blessed *in Abram*. Eventually, all peoples will be blessed by Abram's offspring. At Babel, the Lord scattered the peoples. Now in the promise to Abram, the Lord sets out to gather all nations of the earth. Again, God's mission is global.

The promise of blessing for the nations is repeated to Isaac (Gen. 26:4) and Jacob (Gen. 28:14). The patriarchs, and Israel in them, are chosen in order to be a conduit of God's salvation to all peoples. While this promise will ultimately be fulfilled by Christ and those who receive his commission to make disciples of all nations, we are going to observe smaller fulfillments throughout the rest of the Old Testament. The Lord will bless his people in such a way that it draws men and women from other families and peoples to come to Yahweh in faith. We will see the Lord care for, provide for, and indeed bless Israel with the result that it will issue in redemption for some of these nations of the earth.

While I have highlighted the global nature of God's intended salvation plan, it is important to note that land is one of the blessings promised to Abram. Just as the Lord set the man and the woman in a garden near Eden, he is going to set his people Israel in the land of Canaan, a garden-like land flowing with milk and honey. The Lord's desire to dwell with his people in a place of beauty, holiness, and provision remains. At this point in the narrative, the land of Canaan is chosen to provide just such a place even while Abram knows that the whole earth will one day be the true holy land (Heb. 11:8–16).

## Mission to the Exodus

In the following chapter, we will look at the exodus event as the quintessential saving act of the Old Testament and what it may teach us about God's mission. But before we finish this chapter, we want to observe how the promises to Abram (now Abraham) are experienced in the lives of the patriarchs and those around them. Said another way, how does the blessing of God create a people able to witness to his goodness?

Immediately following God's call, Abraham begins to be blessed. This results in some surrounding nations responding in hostility, but others in covenant friendship. Those nations who link themselves to the patriarchs share in the blessing. Following the blessing of Melchizedek, king of Salem, in Genesis 14, Abraham (Gen. 21:22–23)—and later Isaac (Gen. 26:28–29)—is invited into covenant with Abimelech explicitly because of God's blessing.

Others find themselves swept up into God's blessing in less-than-ideal ways. The Lord will even use the sin of Judah in Genesis 38 to bring the Gentile woman Tamar into the lineage of King David and, eventually, the Messiah, Jesus. And perhaps that is the point—namely, that the Lord is at work through his promises to draw men and women to himself even in the midst of a sinful world and through a sinful people.

One obviously positive example of the patriarchs blessing the nations is the service of Joseph in the court of Pharaoh, which saves not only Israel but also the nations who stream to Egypt from the ends of the earth (Gen. 41:57). Here, the progression is clear. God blesses Joseph (Gen. 39:2, 21–23) even while in prison, to the end that he is made second-in-command to Pharaoh. God further blesses everything that Joseph accomplishes, which overflows to blessing for Israel, Egypt, and many nations. The pharaoh we encounter at the end of Genesis attaches himself to God's people, blessing Joseph and his brothers. And the blesser is blessed in return.

But in Exodus 1, we encounter a pharaoh "who did not know Joseph." This is a comment not so much about his memory but about his heart. He will not bless God's people but curse them. This pharaoh will bring about such a profound judgment on himself and Egypt, and such a marvelous rescue for Israel, that the rest of the Bible will refer to it as the model, the exemplar of God's salvation through judgment.

# 4

# Yahweh Saves

As the book of Exodus opens, we discover Israel in the land of Egypt experiencing the fulfillment of many of the promises of blessing. "The people of Israel were fruitful and increased greatly; they multiplied and grew exceedingly strong, so that the land was filled with them" (1:7). This blessing of growth echoes the original mandate of Genesis 1:28, as well as Genesis 12:1–3. For the first seven verses in Exodus, all seems right with the world. Unfortunately, the new pharaoh of Egypt responds to this blessing by becoming a curse to the people of God. If God is to keep his promise to Abraham, it will only be a matter of time before the Lord brings curses upon this new enemy.

We will see that the exodus is a type, one that will find its antitype in the cross of Christ and the salvation it has purchased for God's people. The exodus narrative shows the helplessness of God's people, their groaning, and their need for deliverance. Just like the gospel, it is a one-way deliverance that depends solely on the grace of God. Even as many Israelites ache for Egypt and groan for their former days in captivity, God reveals himself in mighty acts to redeem a people for himself. The exodus is a picture of salvation, a salvation through blood and water (Ex. 12:7; 14:22). Exodus is a book about a deliverance that comes through revelation and for communion. Let's explore these two facets.

## That My Name May Be Proclaimed in All the Earth

One major aim of the book of Exodus is to reveal the character of God. As one recent biblical-theological work says in its title, the book of Exodus is about *The God Who Makes Himself Known*.[1] In fact, W. Ross Blackburn argues, following Walter Brueggemann, that "the whole book of Exodus is concerned with explaining God's name,"[2] because God's name signifies his very nature. Understanding God's name means knowing God himself. And knowing God *is* eternal life (John 17:3). Therefore, God making himself known is another way of saying God's mission is revelation for communion. Let's see how this plays out in Exodus.

Following the introductory two chapters chronicling the woes of Israel, the Lord begins to reveal himself. This first occurs at the burning bush, where the Lord reveals himself to Moses as the God of Abraham, Isaac, and Jacob. Furthermore, if the Israelites want to know who this God is, Moses is to tell them that he is "I AM" and that the Lord Yahweh has heard their cries and will rescue them (Ex. 3:14–15). Why is this verification necessary? Do the Israelites want to authenticate that the God Moses has encountered is indeed their God? Or is it possible that Israel no longer knows the God of their fathers? Perhaps living in the land of Egypt and dabbling in its idolatry, they have forgotten the true and living God. There is evidence to suggest that the latter is sadly the case (Josh. 24:14). Israel needs to meet God anew.

---

1. W. Ross Blackburn, *The God Who Makes Himself Known: The Missionary Heart of the Book of Exodus*, NSBT 28 (Downers Grove, IL: InterVarsity Press, 2012).

2. Blackburn, *God Who Makes Himself Known*, 34–35.

This God gives signs to Moses so that the people "may believe that the LORD, the God of their fathers, the God of Abraham, the God of Isaac, and the God of Jacob, has appeared" (Ex. 4:5). The signs are meant to reveal God, and the people are meant to trust what they see (Ex. 4:6–9). And why send Moses to the people? So that he may speak as the mouth of God (Ex. 4:14–16). God reveals himself through the works and words he gives to Moses.

But there is a problem. The new pharaoh has forgotten not only Joseph but also the Lord. "Who is the LORD, that I should obey his voice and let Israel go? I do not know the LORD, and moreover, I will not let Israel go" (Ex. 5:2). There is some speculation over whether this means that he has, indeed, not heard of the God of the Israelites or that this is a refusal to recognize the Lord's authority. Given the attention he has paid to Israel in his hard dealings with them, the former seems unlikely. No, his heart is already hardened against Israel and their God.

## The Ten Plagues

How does God respond to the ignorance of Pharaoh? By displaying his supremacy. God will reveal himself: "Now you shall see what I will do" (Ex. 6:1). Everyone will see: "The Egyptians shall know that I am the LORD" (Ex. 7:5). Pharaoh will know (Ex. 7:17). The Egyptian pantheon will have to acknowledge the Lord's supremacy (Num. 33:4). Finally, many other nations will recognize that he is God (Ex. 9:16). All of this will come about through plagues.

In Exodus 9, between the sixth and seventh plagues, the Lord reveals his purpose for the mounting devastation. Indeed, he knows he could have executed deliverance for his people in a single moment (v. 15). But instead he heaps up wonder after wonder like the stones of a pyramid. When Pharaoh considers releasing Israel, the Lord hardens or fortifies Pharaoh's heart so that he refuses to do so

(v. 12). Why? Verse 16 says, "But for this purpose I have raised you up, to show you my power, so that my name may be proclaimed in all the earth." By multiplying his miracles against Egypt, the Lord is also multiplying the revelation of his character to a now watching world. He wants the ends of the earth to know him.

Notice the kind intention of God embedded in these plagues. These awful wonders should shock onlookers so that they might flee to the mountains of God's mercy. These verses are designed to wake up the drowsy man and dull woman stumbling their way to an eternal plague. For the Bible reader today who fails to acknowledge God, who loves his or her sin and the god of the flesh, these plagues are signposts pointing to the plague of hell to come, a place of weeping and gnashing of teeth (Matt. 13:42, 50), where the worm does not die and the fire is never quenched (Mark 9:48). Throughout the book of Revelation we see the repetition and escalation of these plagues from Egypt, from darkness to boils to hail to locusts to water turned to blood (see esp. Rev. 9 and 16). In Revelation 18:4 we read,

> Come out of her, my people,
>> lest you take part in her sins,
> lest you share in her plagues.

Just as many peoples would see the signs in Egypt and turn to the Lord for deliverance (Ex. 12:38), we should read of these dreadful judgments, culminating in an eternal hell, and attach ourselves to the people of God's promise, the church.

Nearly every encounter with the Lord in these chapters of Exodus includes some form of the acknowledgment formula: "you/they/he will know that I am the LORD/God." Rolf Rendtorff writes, "The ever more acerbic dispute as the plagues escalate has one major aim: to bring about an acknowledgment of Yhwh."[3] Repeatedly, the Lord makes it clear that what he is doing in the exodus is revealing himself so that he will be acknowledged as God. In fact, it could be argued that the best way to understand the divine name Yahweh is to fill it up with what he reveals throughout Exodus. If you want to know who this God is, watch what he will do. He is the idol-destroying, pride-spurning, creation-ruling deliverer of the weak and the needy. He is who he is. This may also clarify how the Lord could say that Abraham did not know him in the way Israel would in the exodus (Ex. 6:3).

Those who harden their hearts and turn away will face judgment. But for those who turn to the Lord, acknowledging that he is God— whether Jew, Egyptian, or another watching nation—there will be deliverance through judgment for communion. And that is the point of God's self-disclosure in the exodus—namely, to win a people for himself by magnifying his name.

## My Treasured Possession

While the Israelites may have forgotten God, he has not forgotten them. How could he? His mission has not changed. In the rescue of Israel, we hear echoes of the creation of Adam and Eve and the world, of the rescue of Noah, and of the call of Abraham. God is continuing his work of creating and redeeming a people who will share in the life of God as his sons just as he intended from the beginning.

This redemption is instigated as the Lord remembers his covenant with Abraham, Isaac, and Jacob. These are *his* people; therefore, he hears their cries and will keep his promise (Ex. 2:24; 3:15–16). And so God's message to Pharaoh is spoken in familial terms: "Thus

---

3. Rolf Rendtorff, *The Canonical Hebrew Bible: A Theology of the Old Testament*, trans. David E. Orton (Leiden: Deo, 2005), 472.

says the LORD, 'Israel is my firstborn son,' and I say to you, 'Let my son go that he may serve me. If you refuse to let him go, behold, I will kill your firstborn son'" (Ex. 4:22–23).

In Exodus 6:7, the Lord says to Israel, "I will take you to be my people, and I will be your God, and you shall know that I am the LORD your God, who has brought you out from under the burdens of the Egyptians." This is the result of the mighty deliverance promised in the previous verse. Redeemed for relationship. Recall Exodus 9:16 and the promise that God's mighty acts will result in his name being made known in all the earth. Here the same idea emerges. Revealing the name, making it known in all the earth, means rescue and communion for people. This is the connection between our two themes of revelation and communion. They are further linked in the song of Moses in Exodus 15.

## The Song of Moses

Standing on the shore of the Red Sea, having seen the Lord's mighty defeat of their enemies, Moses and the people sing a song of praise. The bulk of the song in Exodus 15 is taken up with declaring the revelatory acts of God against Egypt, our first theme. On the one hand, the Lord is a man of war depicted as fighting hand-to-hand combat with the enemy (vv. 3–6). On the other, he is revealed as a typhoon, devastating the enemy as the breath of his nostrils manipulates and weaponizes the sea itself. Who is this God? He is the Lord! The song begins and ends with an emphatic accent that he is the only God. He has triumphed gloriously (v. 1); he will reign forever and ever (v. 18).

It is interesting how that theme is punctuated with our second theme of communion. We see this, first, in the possessive pronouns used in verse 2. It seems that Israel has finally caught on with what God is doing. They sing,

> The LORD is my strength and my song,
>> and he has become my salvation;
> this is my God, and I will praise him,
>> my father's God, and I will exalt him.

Though the Lord has spoken of *his people* throughout the book, Israel only now calls him "my God . . . , my father's God." Further, they finally know his name. In verse 3 they sing,

> The LORD is a man of war;
>> the LORD is his name."

In verse 13, following nine verses detailing the Lord's victory, we read,

> You have led in your steadfast love the people whom you
>> have redeemed;
>> you have guided them by your strength to your holy
>>> abode.

This highlights the Lord's purpose toward his people. He worked wonders in Egypt so that he might lead Israel, in steadfast love, eventually to a place where he might dwell with them.

Similarly, verse 17 tells us what the Lord intends for the people he has redeemed:

> You will bring them in and plant them on your own
>> mountain,
>> the place, O LORD, which you have made for your
>>> abode,
>> the sanctuary, O LORD, which your hands have
>>> established.

The Lord has redeemed his people so that he might plant them in a place where he will dwell with them. In each of these segments of the song of Moses in Exodus 15, we see a move from revelatory redemptive activity to relationship. It could be portrayed as shown in table 1.

*Table 1. Movement from redemption to relationship in Exodus 15*

| Redemption | Relationship |
|---|---|
| 2a: "The LORD . . . has become my *salvation*;" | 2b: "this is *my* God, . . . my father's God." |
| 13a: "You have led in your steadfast love the people whom you have *redeemed*;" | 13b: "you have guided them by your strength *to your holy abode*." |
| 16b: ". . . till the people pass by whom you have *purchased*." | 17: "You will bring them in and plant them on your own mountain, the place, O LORD, which you have made for your abode." |

## To Wed and to Witness

The rescue of Israel leads ultimately through the sea to the mountain of God. There at Sinai the Lord enters into a marriage-like covenant with Israel.[4] The Lord makes clear his intentions for Israel in Exodus 19:3–6:

> Thus you shall say to the house of Jacob, and tell the people of Israel: "You yourselves have seen what I did to the Egyptians, and how I bore you on eagles' wings and brought you to myself. Now therefore, if you will indeed obey my voice and keep my covenant, you shall be my treasured possession among all peoples, for all the earth is mine; and you shall be to me a kingdom of priests and a holy nation." These are the words that you shall speak to the people of Israel.

The bracketed repetition of "you shall say/speak" clarifies that these words carry significant freight. The Lord saved Israel so that they

---

4. He constitutes an intimate, one-another, exclusive relationship with his people, which is described in terms of marriage when faithfully kept (Ps. 45; Song of Songs; Ezek. 16:1–14), and adultery when broken (Jer. 3:9; Ezek. 23:27; Hos. 1:2).

might have a unique, exclusive relationship with God. It is marked by intimacy, for the Lord "bore you on eagles' wings and brought you to" himself. They are now his "treasured possession." And just as the Lord called Adam to image God in the world and chose Abraham to funnel blessing to the world, the Israelites are called to serve as priests for the world, bringing God to mankind and bringing humanity to God.

T. Desmond Alexander points out that the Passover mirrors the later ritual for the ordination of the Aaronic priests, with the implication that the Passover consecrates the whole people as priests to God.[5] From blood to hyssop to eating the sacred meat and burning the leftovers, the markers of the later ceremony are all here in the Passover, if worded slightly differently. That the Levites were also substituted for the firstborn of the other tribes indicates this as well. The point is that the Lord is setting apart all his people to be a kingdom of priests for the world.

This priesthood is to bear witness to the world. This is exactly the way Peter later defines the role of a priestly kingdom now held by Jew and Gentile in the church: "But you are a chosen race, a royal priesthood, a holy nation, a people for his own possession, that you may proclaim the excellencies of him who called you out of darkness into his marvelous light" (1 Pet. 2:9). Grammatically, God's people are set apart *in order that* they will proclaim God's excellencies. Karen Jobes rightly argues that God's priestly people are to "make known what God has done, displaying his power, grace, and mercy."[6]

Israel's ability to serve as witnessing priests rests on the revelation and redemption they have just experienced. That is, they can now declare the Lord to the nations, the saving power of the one true

---

5. T. Desmond Alexander, *From Eden to the New Jerusalem: An Introduction to Biblical Theology* (Grand Rapids, MI: Kregel, 2008), 127–30.

6. Karen H. Jobes, *1 Peter*, BECNT (Grand Rapids, MI: Baker Academic, 2005), 163.

God. They have a song to sing of the good God who redeems men and women. Jethro hears the song (Ex. 18:11) and joins the singing. Forty years later, Rahab joins the choir of the redeemed because of the Lord's revelatory redemption in the exodus event (Josh. 2:8–14). Indeed a "mixed multitude" forsake their country, their kindred, and their father's house—following in the steps of their father by faith, Abraham—and go with Israel through the sea and wilderness into the promised land (Ex. 12:38). Gentiles will join themselves to Israel because of what the Lord has done for his people.

## The Reception of the Exodus Event

Much more could be said about revelation for communion in the book of Exodus and the rest of the Pentateuch, but I have tried to zero in on the exodus event itself, from the enslavement of Israel to their arrival at Sinai. In Sinai, the Lord will reveal himself further to his people. They will hear his voice and see his glory, which only further cements what we have already seen—namely, that the Lord reveals himself to make it possible to dwell with his people in committed relationship, hence the need for the law, the tabernacle, the priesthood, and so on.

How is this deliverance understood later in the canon? Consider as one example the way in which Isaiah uses the exodus event in Isaiah 43. Here, the Lord promises a future exodus deliverance for the people of God, following exile. Verses 16–21 boom with reverberations of exodus, including the Lord making a way through the sea (v. 16) and destroying the Egyptian army (v. 17), as well as providing water in the wilderness (v. 20) and forming Israel into a people who will know God and glorify him (vv. 20–21). Isaiah is clear, there will be another exodus. But how will it come about? The Lord will reveal himself to his people and the watching nations once again.

## DIVINE REVELATION

The repetition of the "I am" statements in Isaiah 43:3, 5, 10, 11, 12, 13, 15, 19, and 25 highlights the revelation of the nature of God in this chapter by using the same formula first encountered in Exodus 3. The Lord is refreshing the memory of his people, who again have forsaken him. Seven of these statements end with "Lord," "God," or the enigmatic "he." "I am the Lord," "I am God," "I am he." The Lord could have as easily said: "I am who I am. I am the God of the first exodus making myself known to deliver once again." The Lord will bring back his people through renewed divine revelation, a second exodus.

## FOR COMMUNION

As the Lord reveals himself again in a new exodus, what will be the result?

> But now thus says the Lord,
>> he who created you, O Jacob,
>> he who formed you, O Israel:
> "Fear not, for I have redeemed you;
>> I have called you by name, you are mine.
> When you pass through the waters, I will be with you;
>> and through the rivers, they shall not overwhelm you;
> when you walk through fire you shall not be burned,
>> and the flame shall not consume you.
> For I am the Lord your God,
>> the Holy One of Israel, your Savior.
> I give Egypt as your ransom,
>> Cush and Seba in exchange for you.
> Because you are precious in my eyes,
>> and honored, and I love you,

I give men in return for you,

> peoples in exchange for your life.

Fear not, for I am with you;

> I will bring your offspring from the east,

> and from the west I will gather you.

I will say to the north, Give up,

> and to the south, Do not withhold;

bring my sons from afar

> and my daughters from the end of the earth,

everyone who is called by my name,

> whom I created for my glory,

> whom I formed and made." (Isa. 43:1–7)

Notice the tender language in these verses:[7] "Fear not." "I am with you." "You are mine." "You are precious . . . , and I love you." The Holy One of Israel has lost what is most precious to him, and so he purposes to redeem his sons and daughters again. Because of his great love, the Lord will gather his people to himself. He has formed them for himself. This was the purpose of the first exodus, and it is the purpose of the second, future exodus in the latter days.

Within Exodus itself, the relationship between God and his people is described in a variety of ways. David J. A. Clines lists four: blessing, presence, guidance, and a "continuance of God's relationship with former patriarchs."[8] Each of these categories of relationship is present in Isaiah 43 as well. We see the Lord *blessing* his people through paying a ransom for them (v. 4) and in gathering them back to the land (v. 5). His *presence* is promised to them. He will be with them through the water and in the fire (v. 2). Related to that, his presence will *guide* his people back, saying in effect, "I will bring you"

---

7. One can see a similar reality in Hos. 2:14–23, except the relational picture between the Lord and his people is that of marriage.

8. David J. A. Clines, *Theme of the Pentateuch* (Sheffield: Sheffield Academic, 2001), 35–36.

through the waters and into the land (vv. 2, 5–6). Finally, by addressing the people as "Jacob" and "Israel," the Lord makes it abundantly clear that he is acting in continued covenant faithfulness with the *patriarchs*.

## Exodus as the Sign of Mission

We considered in chapters 1 and 2 the purpose behind God's mission. In creation and redemption, God intends to bring men and women into the fellowship shared by Father, Son, and Spirit. Chapter 3 demonstrated that this mission would be accomplished by the seed of Eve, the offspring of Abraham, and that salvation would be accomplished for all the nations as they are justified by faith in Christ. In the current chapter, I have argued that God's saving work, in the past as well as in the latter days, is accomplished through the revelatory deliverance of God and results in the formation of a people in communion with God. The first exodus was a sign pointing to a future, global, and eternal exodus when God is revealed as our Passover Lamb (John 1:29; 1 Cor. 5:7).

# 5

# Land and Exile

The importance of creation through the exodus event for defining mission is virtually uncontested, even if we may differ here and there in terms of application. When we arrive at the borders of the promised land, however, there is a great divergence of opinion on what the rest of the Old Testament teaches us about God's mission.

Because of the redemptive-historical approach I am following, I believe that God's mission is defined, more or less, by the time we reach Genesis 12:1–3. It will be nuanced more in later books, but God has not wasted time revealing his plan for the world. The exodus, then, shows us what redemption looks like. It is a type of the greater salvation to come.

What we observe in the rest of the Old Testament is the Lord keeping his promises he has already made, and Israel failing to keep covenant and join God's mission in the world. In short, this is the period of the old covenant in which Israel's faithfulness to God waxes and wanes, in which his name is variously magnified and maligned among the nations, and in which we wait for the ultimate fulfillment of his promise to send the Messiah to conquer Satan, sin, and death.

What does that mean for mission in the rest of the Old Testament? Instead of reading the rest of the Old Testament to know what the mission is, we read it to see how it is played out in the lives of God's people and the nations surrounding them. When we do that, one of the things we learn is that God has given gifts to Israel to enable them to be his witnesses to the surrounding world. Unfortunately, we also quickly observe that Israel will fail to deploy those gifts meant to help herald salvation to the nations.

The gifts we will focus on are the law, the temple, and the kingdom. Each of these is given or promised by the end of the Pentateuch. The books of Moses also tell us that we can expect God to keep his promises and Israel to turn away from God and lose the privilege of these gifts. That is what happens, and the Old Testament closes with the promise that each of these gifts will be restored in the latter days through the true and better Moses, Aaron, and David; that is, through the Messiah.

## The Law and Mission

On the plains surrounding Sinai, the Lord covenants with his people. And what does covenant life look like? It looks like righteousness and peace. Like life lived under the law. And living according to the law of God has missional implications. It is a gift to Israel, but it also has witnessing power. As the people approach the promised land, Moses is preparing them to enter it as those who will be faithful to the living God. After summarizing their forty years in the wilderness, he reiterates the importance of the law for them. In Deuteronomy 4:5–8, we read of the impact the law will have on the nations surrounding Israel:

> See, I have taught you statutes and rules, as the LORD my God
> commanded me, that you should do them in the land that you

are entering to take possession of it. Keep them and do them, for that will be your wisdom and your understanding in the sight of the peoples, who, when they hear all these statutes, will say, "Surely this great nation is a wise and understanding people." For what great nation is there that has a god so near to it as the LORD our God is to us, whenever we call upon him? And what great nation is there, that has statutes and rules so righteous as all this law that I set before you today?

By keeping these statutes and rules, Israel will be, as Meredith Kline puts it, "a light to the nations."[1] In particular, keeping the law will allow the nations to understand the wisdom, righteousness, and nearness of the Lord. It all starts with Israel embracing the law, for the law itself will be Israel's wisdom and understanding in the sight of the peoples. It will demonstrate what a flourishing life, a discerning life, looks like.

As Israel lives according to the law, the nations will also begin to make deeper discoveries about Israel's God. First, they will discover that the Lord is near to his people. This law, after all, was delivered "in person" on Mount Sinai, in cloud and fire and lightning. This law outlines how God will tabernacle, or dwell, with his people. The nations will be exposed to the reality of the presence of God on the earth.

And as they hear of the wisdom and nearness of God, they will also realize that he is a righteous God. Moses anticipates this when he asks in verse 8, "What great nation is there, that has statutes and rules so righteous as all this law that I set before you today?" When the nations surrounding Israel hear their own practices condemned in the law, when they hear their own deities exposed by the law, when

---

1. Meredith G. Kline, *The Treaty of the Great King: The Covenant Structure of Deuteronomy* (Grand Rapids, MI: Eerdmans, 1963), 59.

the light of God's holiness shines on their own religion and life, they will know that the Lord is the righteous God.

Eugene Merrill helps us understand the outcome of this righteous living: "This, of course, was part of the attraction of Israel by which they were to become a means of blessing the whole earth."[2] Care for the needy (e.g., Deut. 15:7–11), just politics (e.g., Deut. 17:14–20), righteous business practices (e.g., Deut. 25:13–16), and especially right worship (e.g., Deut. 16:21–17:7) all speak to the nations around them who practice unrighteousness in every area of life. Then, as today, the truth of God proclaimed is the fragrance of death to those who are perishing but life to those who are being saved. We see this displayed in the visit of the queen of Sheba in 1 Kings 10, for she "heard of the fame of Solomon concerning the name of the LORD" (v. 1).

Notice how Solomon's wisdom—in accord with faithful obedience to the law, which issues in his righteous rule and prosperity— witnesses to the truth of God to her. For she comes because of what she has heard "concerning the name of the LORD." The result of seeing the wisdom (vv. 2–4) and the nearness of God (v. 5), is to cry out, breathlessly, "Blessed be the LORD your God, who has delighted in you and set you on the throne of Israel" (v. 9). One of the purposes of the law and the law-dependent principles we find in Proverbs is to display the character, the name, of God so that men and women would be drawn to the Lord and be saved.

## Temple and Mission

How might the temple, the place of God's dwelling with his people, be a gift to Israel that would draw the nations to the Lord? Solomon provides an answer in 1 Kings 8. As he dedicates the temple to the Lord through prayer, we read in verses 41–43:

---

2. Eugene H. Merrill, *Deuteronomy*, NAC 4 (Nashville: Broadman and Holman, 1994), 117.

Likewise, when a foreigner, who is not of your people Israel, comes from a far country for your name's sake (for they shall hear of your great name and your mighty hand, and of your outstretched arm), when he comes and prays toward this house, hear in heaven your dwelling place and do according to all for which the foreigner calls to you, in order that all the peoples of the earth may know your name and fear you, as do your people Israel, and that they may know that this house that I have built is called by your name.

Notice that Solomon assumes that foreigners will come for the sake of God's name—that is, because of what they hear about the character of the God of Israel. Paul House observes. "Solomon knows that all nations need to know the Lord and that Israel must mediate this knowledge."[3] So foreigners must hear of his great name and mighty hand. Not only the wisdom and righteousness of the law but also the greatness and power of God will draw people who want to be near to God because of the witness of Israel.

Perhaps the greatest missional impact of the temple is the worship held in its courts daily. The Psalms repeatedly unfold God's missional agenda for his people. First, the Psalms teach the supremacy of God, thus rendering all competitors worthless and helpless, whether idols (96:4–5; 97:7) or kingdoms (2; 33:10). Second, they call Israel to witness to the nations concerning God's glory, salvation, and reign (96:1–3, 10). The language used in Psalm 96, for instance, in "tell of his salvation," is the Hebrew equivalent to proclaiming the good news or declaring the gospel in the New Testament. This, says Walter Kaiser, is the same language used in "important eschatological and soteriological texts such as Isaiah 40:9; 41:27; 52:7; and 61:1" to describe the witness of God's people in the

---

3. Paul R. House, *1, 2 Kings*, NAC 8 (Nashville: Broadman and Holman, 1995), 146.

latter days.[4] Third, we see the psalmists not only exhort Israel to praise the Lord before the nations but also model this in their own writing (Pss. 18:49; 57:9). Fourth, we see the certainty that, indeed, the nations will come and worship the one true and living God (Pss. 22:27; 46:10).

In Psalm 67 the psalmist asks the Lord to bless Israel so that the nations of the earth would know him. In that way, Psalm 67 is a poetic commentary on Genesis 12:1–3.[5] Just as blessing was promised to Abram *so that* all the peoples on earth would be blessed, the psalmist's request for blessing has a purpose to it. He borrows from the Aaronic blessing, speaking it in the first person and extending it, as it were, to all nations. Psalm 67:1 asks for blessing, and the first line of verse 2 describes the purpose of this blessing: "that your way may be known on earth." The goal of the requested blessing is that God be made known, that he be acknowledged by all the nations.

The psalmist, in effect, is asking God to reveal himself in such a way that the nations would come to know him. He desires that the nations worship God, that they fear God (67:4–5, 7). The psalmist aligns himself with God's own desire—namely, that his revelation would result in communion with all the nations of the earth. Verse 7 repeats the request for blessing and the purpose of that blessing as redemption for the nations.[6]

It is intriguing to recall that Psalm 67 was often sung during the celebration of Pentecost. This psalm certainly asks for and celebrates the provision of harvest, but it is also pointing to a greater harvest, a different sort of harvest (John 4:35). One can almost imagine the early church gathered in Jerusalem, waiting as Jesus has told them to

---

4. Walter C. Kaiser, *Mission in the Old Testament: Israel as a Light to the Nations* (Grand Rapids, MI: Baker, 2000), 34n5.

5. Derek Kidner, *Psalms 1–72*, TOTC (Downers Grove, IL: InterVarsity Press, 1971), 236.

6. V. 7 may also be rendered as expressing result instead of purpose: "God shall bless us, with the result that all the ends of the earth fear him."

do, singing this psalm even as the Spirit of mission descends on them and accomplishes the requests of Psalm 67 on the day of Pentecost.

## Kingdom and Mission

The promise of a king who will reign for the good of God's people begins in Genesis 17:6, and the vision of a king from the tribe of Judah who will rule the nations takes sharp focus at the end of Genesis (49:8–12). During the oracles of Balaam, we find that the seed of Abraham is also the lion of Judah (see esp. Num. 24:5–9). He will be a king who saves. The Lord will eventually place a man of his own choosing on the throne of Israel. That man's administration is meant to be a witness to Israel and the nations, pointing to the eventual Savior-King who will come.

The well-known account of David and Goliath in 1 Samuel gives us a picture of this witness. The fact that this narrative follows directly after David's anointing in chapter 16 should alert us to something theologically significant. In chapter 17, God's newly anointed king goes out to save God's people. Together, these chapters reveal what God's messianic King will be like.

The author of 1 Samuel takes special pains to emphasize the importance of this narrative. From its total length to the thorough dialogue to the sharing of minute details typically omitted, the author wants the reader's full attention.[7] At the center of the story is a battle between the Philistines' "champion" (Heb.: "the man between") and Israel's, two representatives for their people. The fate of the champion would be the fate of the entire army.

What is clear in the wider passage is that the Israelite army is helpless in the face of such a warrior as Goliath. They cannot save themselves; indeed, they are on the verge of fleeing (17:11, 16, 24).

---

7. For a brief introduction to some of these techniques employed by the author, see Robert D. Bergen, *1, 2 Samuel*, NAC 7 (Nashville: Broadman and Holman, 1996), 187–88.

Much like the exodus, it's not God's people who "go on mission" to save the day. No, they needed a savior, a champion, a man to stand between them and the enemy. And David claims that he is uniquely suited for the role. How so? He argues that he knows how to lay his life down for the sheep (17:31–37). In one sense, this passage is missional in that it prefigures the deliverance of God's people by the coming Savior-seed who will lay his life down for the salvation of all nations, the good shepherd. The reader of this passage should recognize its antitype in Christ (John 10:1–18). In that way—in David's Christlike rescue—witness is given.

In another sense, we also see verbal witness. David is under no delusion of his own capacity. Indeed, whether addressing the fearful Israelites (1 Sam. 17:37) or the defiant giant, Goliath (17:45–47), David is adamant that the battle belongs to the Lord. God is the ultimate deliverer. And what is the result? David says that the Lord will be acknowledged; the Lord will be revealed and known. His supremacy will be displayed. In fact, after this battle, "all the earth may know that there is a God in Israel" (17:46). Echoes of the deliverance from Egypt, especially Exodus 9:6, run through this narrative. The Lord will save in power, and the nations will acknowledge him.

## Blessings Abused and Failed Witness

We have seen how law, temple, and kingdom are meant as good gifts from God, which, when practiced and stewarded according to God's word, produce a witnessing effect among the nations. Unfortunately, often these gifts are abused by Israel, resulting not in drawing the nations but in repulsing them.

When the *law* is broken, the name of the Lord is not magnified but maligned (Jer. 32:34; Ezek. 43:8). Therefore, God will act for the sake of his name (Ezek. 20), bringing curses against his people to discipline them (Deut. 28:15–68). When this happens, the nations then will ask, "Why did this happen?" and the Lord's holiness will be vindicated. For it is made clear that the judgment is due to Israel's faithlessness, not due to the failure of the Lord (Deut. 29:24–28). Instead, even as he judges Israel, he will be seen as holy.

When the *temple* is eventually left in disrepair or worse, filled with idols (Ezek. 8–9), the Lord will remove his nearness from Israel. The presence of God dwelling with his people, which formerly drew the nations to Jerusalem, departs the temple (Ezek. 10:18), which is eventually destroyed by the Babylonians (2 Kings 25:9).

The *kingdom* of Israel peaks during the first half of Solomon's reign. Yet, within one generation, the kingdom is split. Graeme Goldsworthy is helpful here as he argues that following the idolatry of Solomon, the son of David, the narrative of the Old Testament begins a downward trajectory that can only end in exile. Even as kings continued to reign, the promise of the real, eschatological kingdom of the true Son of David is emerging as a significant prophetic theme.[8]

All three gifts are abused and eventually lost. Yet all three are taken up in prophetic discourse. Along with the return to the land following exile, Israel is promised that they will become *law keepers* with access to the presence of God in the *temple*,[9] living under the good reign of *David's Son*. It is no coincidence, then, that when Israel experiences that restoration in the latter days,[10] there will also be a great ingathering of the nations (e.g., Isa. 2:2–3/Mic. 4:1–2; Zech. 8:18–22).

These themes of restored obedience, presence/temple, and kingdom in the latter days are found together in the latter prophets, from

---

8. While Goldsworthy has addressed this in many places, the most comprehensive treatment is Graeme Goldsworthy, *The Goldsworthy Trilogy: Gospel and Kingdom, Gospel and Wisdom, The Gospel in Revelation* (Carlisle, UK: Paternoster, 2000).

9. Or even more wonderful is that the Spirit of God will dwell in them!

10. Indeed, the original promise to Judah and its repetition in the oracles of Balaam are clear that David could never have been the lion of Judah, but that a latter-days King would reign forever.

Isaiah to Malachi. One brief example: following the vision of the valley of dry bones in Ezekiel 37, we hear of the Lord bringing his people back to the land (v. 21), united into one kingdom (vv. 15–22), obeying the law of the Lord (v. 24), dwelling in the presence of God (vv. 26–27), under the rule of David (vv. 24–25). What will be the result of this restoration of Israel? What will happen among the nations when the Lord reveals his glory and goodness again? The very next verse, and the final verse in the oracle, says, "Then the nations will know that I am the Lord who sanctifies Israel, when my sanctuary is in their midst forevermore" (v. 28). The nations will acknowledge the Lord. They will see the gifts of God restored to his people, again demonstrating his nearness and holiness, and they will acknowledge that he is God.

The order here is important to notice. The restoration begins when the Lord regenerates his people. They are dead. They need to be made alive. Until that happens, they are helpless. Reflect again on the reigns of David and Solomon. The people of Israel were in the land, they had the law, they had God's appointed king, and they had rest from their enemies. If any people ever had the capacity to establish the kingdom of God through physical means, it was Israel. But within one generation they turned to wholesale idolatry. The old enemies—Satan, sin, and death—had not been dealt with.

The order is important because when we think of the mission of the church today, it is easy to confuse the fruit of the mission with the mission itself. We may confuse working for societal peace, well-being, and prosperity as the mission. Israel had all those things and more under David. But they were not yet regenerated. God's mission is a spiritual mission before anything else.

We have spent this chapter recognizing the missional impact of fruitful lives and righteous rule—that is, societal and political holiness. These things do indeed have a witnessing effect of a kind.

But only those who are regenerated are able to be with God and indeed walk in his ways. When the true Moses, Aaron, and David (the Prophet, Priest, and King) comes to reveal the glory of God in the latter days, the exodus that he will bring about will lead to true transformation, personal and communal, as he establishes an everlasting communion with those who acknowledge the Lord.

## Mission through the Exile

Despite Israel's unfaithfulness, we continue to see God's heart for all peoples throughout the Old Testament. We see this in God's warmhearted concern for Nineveh, despite Jonah's loathing of the Assyrians (Jonah 4:10–11). We see the Lord use even the exile and his faithfulness to his people to stir up belief within the Babylonian and Persian courts. He will even cause their kings—Nebuchadnezzar and Darius, respectively—to witness to the supremacy of the Lord to the many nations and peoples over which they reign. Nebuchadnezzar testifies to the power and goodness of God to "all peoples, nations, and languages, that dwell in all the earth" (Dan. 4:1; see also Dan. 3:25–29); and "Darius wrote to all the peoples, nations, and languages that dwell in all the earth" to promote the fear of the Lord (Dan. 6:25–27). These two pagan kings may have the greatest missional witness of anyone in the Old Testament.

Certainly, the witness of men like Daniel, Shadrach, Meshach, and Abednego stands out during this period; but in general, the message of the prophets is that a time will come when God will give his people new hearts, establish his kingdom through a new David, who will lead a new exodus and establish a new covenant. The Lord himself will do it. God will come and fulfill his mission.

# 6

# The Great Commission

We have now come to the New Testament. As we look back over the Old Testament, we may notice that, in some sense, the mission of God was under way, but we also observe that, in another sense, God's mission was more promised than realized. As a result, there is some continuity and some discontinuity between the Old and New Testaments' displays of this mission.

The continuity we will see is in the activity and purpose of God's mission. In both creation and redemption, God creates a people for relationship through his revelatory work. The discontinuity exists in that God is preparing the world for the time when he will act definitively and finally to redeem a people for himself from all the nations. In the Old Testament, the Lord makes a way to overlook the sins of his people (i.e., the sacrificial system) and he rescues them physically from their enemies. The exodus points to a new exodus. The temple system points to a true atonement. The defeat of evil armies points to the defeat of the real enemies—Satan, sin, and death. Moses, Aaron, and David, as great as each man is, prefigures the true Prophet, Priest, and King. The Lord is preparing the world in the

Old Testament for when the "fullness of time" will come (Gal. 4:4; see also Mark 1:15; Rom. 5:6; Eph. 1:9–10). The world is waiting for the Messiah.

In this chapter, we will focus our attention on Matthew's Gospel, particularly the Great Commission of 28:16–20. The Great Commission is seen by some mission scholars as simply a proof text for global disciple making—a command to obey, yes, but not a passage that should be central to our understanding of the mission of God. I will argue, however, that this passage represents a turning point in redemptive history. Jesus's commission is freighted with all that has come before it in the Old Testament Scriptures. We know from the rest of his Gospel that Matthew is helping us understand how Jesus is bringing fulfillment to all the key Old Testament promises, but we seem to forget this when we come to the Great Commission.

What does this global mandate have to do with the rest of the Gospel and, indeed, the Old Testament? Matthew, I believe, would say, "Everything." In this short passage, Matthew masterfully pulls together the many thematic threads (e.g., God's people, God's kingdom, God's salvation, God's temple, God's victory, God's restoration) woven throughout his Gospel and brings them to bear on the mission of God that now flows out of the supreme revelation of God in the person of Jesus Christ.[1] Matthew also demonstrates how the blessings from our previous chapter—law, temple, and kingdom—are restored to God's people as they witness to the nations. Far from an add-on to his Gospel, the Great Commission is Matthew's summary text to understand how God's mission will come to completion and what it now looks like to join God in his mission as his people.

---

1. R. T. France, *The Gospel of Matthew*, NICNT (Grand Rapids, MI: Eerdmans, 2007), 1106–8.

## The Commission

The disciples have returned to a mountain in Galilee of the Gentiles where Jesus's ministry first began and where they were called to be his disciples. Jesus has sent them here. Here is the account in Matthew's Gospel:

> Now the eleven disciples went to Galilee, to the mountain to which Jesus had directed them. And when they saw him they worshiped him, but some doubted. And Jesus came and said to them, "All authority in heaven and on earth has been given to me. Go therefore and make disciples of all nations, baptizing them in the name of the Father and of the Son and of the Holy Spirit, teaching them to observe all that I have commanded you. And behold, I am with you always, to the end of the age." (28:16–20)

### ALL AUTHORITY IN THE REVEALED SON OF MAN

Jesus first reveals who he is. He is the one with all authority. That is, Jesus is the Son of Man of Daniel 7 and the King of Zechariah 14. Jesus is the one who receives

> . . . dominion
>     and glory and a kingdom,
> that all peoples, nations, and languages
>     should serve him;
> his dominion is an everlasting dominion,
>     which shall not pass away,
> and his kingdom one
>     that shall not be destroyed. (Dan. 7:14)

In Daniel 7, the son of man is given the kingdom by the Father, the "Ancient of Days" (vv. 9, 13). Notice the purpose: "*that* all peoples, nations, and languages should serve him." He will rule, and the nations will stream to serve—that is, to worship—him (Zech. 14:1–17).[2] It is important to note how this is all accomplished. The ruling King of Zechariah 14 is the suffering servant of Zechariah 13.

> "Awake, O sword, against my shepherd,
>> against the man who stands next to me,"
>>> declares the LORD of hosts.
>
> "Strike the shepherd, and the sheep will be scattered."
>> (Zech. 13:7)

The result of this sacrifice is a people, regathered and refined by fire, who will belong to God, and he to them (Zech. 13:9).

Christ's authority, then, flows directly from the cross (see Phil. 2:9: Rev. 5:9). He has authority during his earthly ministry, great authority. But now, after his self-giving sacrifice, he possesses the eschatological authority reserved until the inauguration of the messianic kingdom.[3] This is seen in Revelation 5 as well, for the Lamb that was slain for all peoples is alone worthy (v. 9) to open the scroll of history.

Though God's people abused the gift of kingship in the Old Testament, Jesus has come as the true and better King. The revelation of Christ's blood-bought authority sets the stage for the rest of the commission.

## Go, Therefore, and Make Disciples of All Nations, a New Global People

Matthew has prepared us, throughout his Gospel, for a new Israel—comprising Jew and Gentile. Jesus recapitulates the journey of Is-

---

2. So Peter Stuhlmacher, *Biblical Theology of the New Testament*, trans. Daniel P. Bailey (Grand Rapids, MI: Eerdmans, 2018), 609–10.

3. D. A. Carson, *Matthew*, rev. ed., EBC (Grand Rapids, MI: Zondervan, 2010), 594–95.

rael into Egypt, into the Jordan River, through the wilderness, and
into the promised land (Matt. 1–4) before he ascends a mountain
to deliver the law of God (Matt. 5–7). All of this has led scholars to
argue that Jesus is, now, the new Israel. He then calls twelve disciples
(Matt. 10:1), reflecting the twelve tribes. He sends them out two by
two, reminiscent of the spies sent throughout the land (Mark 6:7;
Luke 10:1). He does battle with God's enemies (e.g., Matt. 12:25–
29), wresting away not land from Canaanites but humanity from
the evil one.

We see the Jewish leaders reject the Messiah (Matt. 23), resulting
in their own rejection. Cursed are those who curse this new Israel.
Now, Matthew tells us, the active and global work of adding the nations to the believers of Israel must commence. The ancient promises
that the nations would be joined to Israel as God's people, his inheri-
tance, are coming to fulfillment (e.g., Isa. 19:25).

The Messiah has purchased a people for God from among the
nations. Because the kingdom has been inaugurated, and Christ has
received all eschatological authority, we stand at the point in redemptive history where the nations must then worship the King. The sur-
prise we encounter, however, is that instead of the nations streaming
to Jerusalem, Jesus sends out his disciples to go to the nations, as he
sits enthroned in heaven.

While "go" is a participle in the original Greek text of Matthew
28:19, it still carries the force of an imperative both grammatically
and logically, for how can disciples be made "of all nations" unless
followers of Jesus go to those nations? The peoples of the earth will
encounter the Messiah not through long caravans journeying to the
Middle East but instead through word and sacrament, as disciples
scatter throughout the world declaring that Jesus is Lord and baptiz-
ing believers into the name of Father, Son, and Spirit. In this overlap
of the ages, the treasure of God is sent out to the nations. Only at

Christ's return, it would seem, will the nations physically stream to Jerusalem, bringing gold and fine gifts. Until then, the King receives gifts of praise and allegiance as men and women are converted and discipled.

Though his own ministry is to the lost sheep of Israel (Matt. 15:24), Jesus regularly ministers to Samaritans and Gentiles. In Matthew's Gospel we see Jesus feeding the four thousand Gentiles (15:32–39), praising the faith of a Roman centurion (8:10) and Canaanite woman (15:28), and so fulfilling the prophecy of the promised one in whom the Gentiles would hope (12:17–21).

The ground is laid for this ministry, a ministry focused on the Jews but generous to Gentiles, in Matthew 1, where we encounter four Gentile women in the genealogy of Jesus. While Matthew may have more than one reason to include these women,[4] we nevertheless see in them a history of God's kindness toward the nations in the Old Testament.

In the Great Commission, God continues with his original plan in Eden, a world filled with men and women who would reflect and represent the good God in all the earth—that is, disciples of all nations. While the gift of law in the Old Testament was abused by God's people, Jesus is gathering a people who will obey all that he commands as they fill the earth as his image-bearing disciples.

## WITH YOU ALWAYS, TO THE END OF THE AGE AS THE PROMISE OF GOD'S CONTINUED PRESENCE

The one named "God with us" (Matt. 1:23) is with us still. The presence of Christ with us, by the Spirit, ensures success in

---

4. Some suggest that the charges of infidelity against Mary the mother of Jesus are refuted through examples of Old Testament women with varying degrees of scandal in their histories. Because Jews of the day see them as legitimate mothers within the Davidic line, so too Mary is vindicated despite the mystery surrounding her pregnancy.

the church's mission in the world. According to Matthew 28:20, the commissioned church has never experienced even the slightest moment when Christ has not been with them. Jesus's presence is perpetual (the entirety of each day) and everlasting ("to the end of the age").

The phrase in 28:20 rendered "the end of the age" appears in two other chapters in Matthew's Gospel. The first is Matthew 13, in the parable of the weeds and the parable of the net, each depicting the final gathering and judgment of humanity at the end of the age. The second is chapter 24, as a part of the Olivet Discourse, when Jesus is asked by his disciples about his return and the "end of the age." Jesus's response in verse 14 represents a clear answer to the disciples' question about the end. There Jesus says, "And this gospel of the kingdom will be proclaimed throughout the whole world as a testimony to all nations, and then the end will come."

While false messiahs and wars are only the beginning, merely birth pains (Matt. 24:8), the sign of the end given by Jesus is the global witness of the gospel. Hoekema argues:

> The missionary preaching of the gospel to all the nations is, in fact, the outstanding and most characteristic sign of the times. It gives to the present age its primary meaning and purpose. The period between Christ's first and second coming is the missionary age *par excellence*. This is a time of grace, a time when God invites and urges all men to be saved. In the Great Commission, in fact, this sign takes the form of a command: "Go therefore and make disciples of all nations."[5]

---

5. Anthony A. Hoekema, *The Bible and the Future* (Grand Rapids, MI: Eerdmans, 1994), 139.

This idea that the last days is a period for global mission is echoed elsewhere in the New Testament.

First, Paul writes in Romans 11:25, "I do not want you to be unaware of this mystery, brothers: a partial hardening has come upon Israel, until the fullness of the Gentiles has come in." Regardless of how one interprets "all Israel" in verse 26, the reality remains the same. There is an era that will last until the "fullness of the Gentiles/nations" is redeemed, and only then will all Israel (whether specifically ethnic Israel or Jew and Gentile united in the church) be saved. Though many will reject Jesus during this time, some Jews will be made jealous as the Lord brings the Gentiles into his family (Rom. 11:11, 14).

Second, Peter's argument in 2 Peter 3:3–12 proceeds along similar lines when he says:

> Scoffers will come in the *last days* with scoffing. . . . They will say, "Where is the promise of his coming? . . ."
>
> But do not overlook this one fact, beloved, that with the Lord one day is as a thousand years, and a thousand years as one day. The Lord is not slow to fulfill his promise as some count slowness, but is patient toward you, not wishing that any should perish, but that all should reach repentance. But *the day of the Lord* will come like a thief. . . .
>
> Since all these things are thus to be dissolved, what sort of people ought you to be in lives of holiness and godliness, waiting for and hastening the coming of the day of God . . . !

Peter here delineates between "the last days," that period of mercy in which the gospel goes out to the nations, and "the day of the Lord," the final day of judgment. We are living in the last days, according to Peter, and we are waiting for the day of the Lord. Peter argues that the second coming is delayed because God is patient, waiting for men and women to hear and believe.

Peter even seems to imply that a global gospel witness is a part of God's divine and sovereign means for "hastening" the return of Christ (v. 12). Said another way, if God is slow to return in order that more people might receive mercy, it is conversely true that should the many repent and be saved, his return would be hastened. How this works, how divine sovereignty and the church's mission interact in this way, is mysterious; nevertheless, the logic holds.

This brings us back to the Great Commission. How long will Jesus empower this mission work with his very presence? To the very end of the age. Mission is *the* end-of-the-age activity. George Eldon Ladd writes that these passages tell us "about the same mission: world-wide evangelization until the end of the Age."[6]

It is important, therefore, to note the connection between God's mission and what is known as inaugurated eschatology, the idea that at his first coming, Jesus inaugurated the kingdom of God, but its consummation waits until his second coming. Inaugurated eschatology explains how many aspects of the kingdom are here and present now, but many other facets wait until the end. We might summarize the major aspects in the following three points:

- There are two stages to the victory of the King. The first stage is the death blow delivered to Satan, sin, and death in his first coming, and the second stage is the full overthrow of these enemies at his second coming. God's people now

---

6. George Eldon Ladd, *The Gospel of the Kingdom: Scriptural Studies in the Kingdom of God* (Grand Rapids, MI: Eerdmans, 1990), 126. For Ladd's unpacking of Matt. 24:14 as giving the church our message, mission, and motive, see 123–40.

have the law written on their hearts, even as we wait for all evil to be obliterated.

- There are two locations to God's restoration. Restoration first occurs internally in the hearts of men and women and will occur externally throughout the entire cosmos after Christ's return. God's presence now dwells within the believer by the Spirit even as we await his presence filling the whole earth as a temple.

- There are two timings in the coming of the King. Jesus came first to deal with sin and will come again to judge the world and to make all things right. The King rules now in the church but will exercise his full reign in all the earth in the age to come.

The point I have developed in this section helps us understand why God orchestrated this twofold kingdom timing. The writer to the Hebrews sums it up succinctly:

> But as it is, he has appeared once for all at the end of the ages to put away sin by the sacrifice of himself. And just as it is appointed for man to die once, and after that comes judgment, so Christ, having been offered once to bear the sins of many, will appear a second time, not to deal with sin but to save those who are eagerly waiting for him. (9:26–28)

Here at the end of the ages, what I have been referring to as the last days, Jesus first came "to put away sin by the sacrifice of himself"— that is, to secure salvation. His second coming, however, will be to execute judgment upon his enemies and bring to himself those who are waiting for him. Logically, what must happen between these two comings so that men and women are "waiting for him"? They must hear the gospel and believe.

Keeping inaugurated eschatology in mind helps us avoid what might be called over-realized missiology. Today we long for global peace and justice, we earnestly desire worldwide equity, we ache for the annihilation of all suffering. But these things are part of the birth pains of the latter days. They will continue until the last day, until Jesus returns and restores the cosmos, gleaming and new. In that day, all evil will be destroyed. In our ministries of justice and mercy, the church reveals something of what Jesus will do in the end, but until then, "This gospel of the kingdom will be proclaimed throughout the whole world as a testimony to all nations, and then the end will come" (Matt. 24:14).

## Commissioned

Let us conclude this chapter by considering what it means that Jesus commissions the disciples, and therefore the church, in Matthew 28:18–20. There is some debate over whether this commissioning follows a formula or pattern developed throughout the Old Testament in the calls of Abraham (Gen. 12:1–3), Moses (Ex. 3), Joshua (Josh. 1:1–11), and prophets like Isaiah (Isa. 6).[7]

I would agree that a pattern can indeed be discerned in the Old Testament, but it is more flexible than recent studies allow.[8] If this is true, the Great Commission may simply be one in a line of biblical commissionings, or, more intriguingly, it constitutes the fulfillment of the Old Testament commissionings. Could the Great Commission be the fulfillment of the call to Moses to lead God's eschatological

---

7. See Carson, *Matthew*, 661–62, for a brief overview.

8. I would argue that, as Rendtorff has convincingly shown that the covenant formula ("You shall be my people, and I will be your God") may appear in part or in whole and yet communicate the fullness of the covenant which these relationships confirm, the presence of some aspects of a commissioning pattern is enough to confirm the existence of the relationship between the Lord and those commissioned, as well as the task for which the commission is given. Rolf Rendtorff, *The Covenant Formula: An Exegetical and Theological Investigation* (Edinburgh: T&T Clark, 1998).

people into his promised land? Is the conquest of Canaan pointing to a better, eternal conquest of all nations led by a greater Joshua? Is the church sent, like Isaiah, in these latter days to speak on behalf of the God who is holy, holy, holy?

There is a connection between Chronicles (the last book in the Hebrew Bible) and Matthew (the first book in the Greek New Testament) that is instructive. Matthew's Gospel begins with a genealogy that partly relies on the genealogy of 1 Chronicles 1–3.[9] Just as the Chronicler begins his book searching for the Messiah to come, Matthew is able to say, "Christ has come." Likewise, 2 Chronicles ends with the return from captivity (36:23), but Matthew will declare that true restoration and the full end of exile has come through Christ and his mission through the church (Matt. 28:18–20). It appears that Matthew is updating the work of 1 and 2 Chronicles in light of the coming of the Messiah and the dawning of the new creation.[10]

In 2 Chronicles 36:23, we read: "Thus says Cyrus king of Persia, 'The LORD, the God of heaven, has given me all the kingdoms of the earth, and he has charged me to build him a house at Jerusalem, which is in Judah. Whoever is among you of all his people, may the LORD his God be with him. Let him go up.'" Table 2 demonstrates the parallels between the commissioning of Cyrus, the Lord's shepherd and messiah (Isa. 44:28–45:1), and the Great Commission of Matthew given by the true shepherd and Messiah.[11]

---

9. France, *Matthew*, 35–36.

10. What follows is built on the work of A. B. Vance in which he demonstrates Matthew's portrayal of Jesus as the end-times temple builder. A. B. Vance, "The Church as the New Temple in Matthew 16:17–19: A Biblical-Theological Consideration of Jesus' Response to Peter's Confession as Recorded by Matthew" (ThM thesis, Gordon-Conwell Theological Seminary, 1992), 9–37.

11. I am indebted to Scott Hafemann for introducing me to Vance's work and much of the makeup of table 2.

*Table 2. Parallel commissions of Cyrus and Jesus*

|  | **2 Chronicles 36:23** | **Matthew 28:18–20** |
| --- | --- | --- |
| Sender | Cyrus, king of Persia | Jesus, the true messianic King |
| Authority | Given all the kingdoms of the earth | Given all authority in heaven and on earth |
| Charge | Build the Lord a house in Jerusalem | Make disciples of all nations |
| Presence | May the Lord be with his people | Jesus is with his people |
| Sending | Let him go up to Jerusalem | Go, therefore, to all nations |

Notice the shared elements in the two passages. Cyrus is king of Persia and given the kingdoms of the earth by God in heaven. Christ, however, is the true King with authority in heaven and on earth. Whereas Cyrus is commissioned to rebuild the temple in Jerusalem, Jesus is building the global temple of God, comprising disciples from all nations. Cyrus blesses the people—"May the LORD his God be with him"—but Christ promises blessing in and through his own perpetual presence.

What instruction ought we to draw from these parallels? If it is the Messiah, the Son of David, who will build the last-days temple of God (2 Sam. 7:12–16), then Matthew's commission is the fulfillment of the Old Testament promises of both temple and restoration. While God's people abuse the gift of the temple, and so it is destroyed, Jesus is building a temple made not of stone but of the redeemed (e.g., 1 Cor. 3:10–17; 2 Cor. 6:16; Eph. 2:19–22), the church. His temple construction is not concerned with a certain mountain in Jerusalem but is a spiritual house of living stones (1 Pet. 2:4–5), among all nations worshiping in spirit and truth (John 4:21–24). Jesus—and through him, the church—is the place to go for the forgiveness of sins (Matt. 9:6), for true temple worship (Matt. 12:6), and for access to God (Matt. 27:51). In short, the Great Commission is the sending of God's people into all nations to build the last-days temple of God.

It is also a fulfillment of the mandate in Eden to be fruitful and multiply and fill the earth—to shape the world into a garden temple.[12] It is the fulfillment of the global promise of blessing through Abraham's seed. It is the true exodus under the prophet like Moses. The return from Babylon in 2 Chronicles was just a picture of the true and better restoration Jesus has commissioned. And that is the story of the rest of the New Testament. It is a story of the Spirit-empowered witness of the church to the saving revelation of God in Christ to the ends of the earth and the end of days.

---

12. G. K. Beale, *The Temple and the Church's Mission: A Biblical Theology of the Dwelling Place of God*, NSBT 17 (Downers Grove, IL: InterVarsity Press, 2004), 176–77.

# 7

# The Church on Mission

In this chapter we will see that God's mission now advances through the testimony of his Spirit-filled church in order to redeem a people for fellowship from all nations.

There is no doubt that Acts is about the mission of God and the church's role in it. Acts has been called the "mission document par excellence"[1] and "the Mount Everest of the biblical theology of mission."[2] I have argued that redemptive history reveals a God-centered mission that has always been heading toward the coming of the Messiah. Now that the Christ has come and has dealt a death blow to the enemies of God—Satan, sin, and death—the ingathering of the nations can begin in earnest.

---

1. J. H. Bavinck, *An Introduction to the Science of Mission*, trans. David H. Freeman (Phillipsburg, NJ: P&R, 1990), 36.
2. Andreas Köstenberger and T. Desmond Alexander, *Salvation to the Ends of the Earth: A Biblical Theology of Mission*, 2nd ed., NSBT 53 (Downers Grove, IL: InterVarsity Press, 2020), 121.

## Luke 24:44–49: Await "Power from on High"

The book of Acts carries on Luke's narrative of what Christ has begun and now continues by his Spirit through his people. Let's notice, first, how Luke ends his Gospel in Luke 24:44–49:

> Then [Jesus] said to them, "These are my words that I spoke to you while I was still with you, that everything written about me in the Law of Moses and the Prophets and the Psalms must be fulfilled." Then he opened their minds to understand the Scriptures, and said to them, "Thus it is written, that the Christ should suffer and on the third day rise from the dead, and that repentance for the forgiveness of sins should be proclaimed in his name to all nations, beginning from Jerusalem. You are witnesses of these things. And behold, I am sending the promise of my Father upon you. But stay in the city until you are clothed with power from on high."

Notice, Jesus is concerned that his disciples understand how he fulfills the Old Testament. He is expounding the Law, Prophets, and Psalms—the Scriptures. In this way, Luke gives us Jesus's one-paragraph summary of the entirety of the Old Testament's teaching about himself *and* what that means for mission. How does he summarize the Old Testament?

First, Jesus says that the Old Testament teaches us about a suffering and rising Messiah—that is, about what Jesus has already accomplished. Jesus's suffering and resurrection, and their fulfillment of the Old Testament, are major themes throughout the book of Acts. At Pentecost, Peter quotes Psalm 16:8–11, stressing the point that the Messiah would suffer but would be vindicated (Acts 2:22–32). We see similar uses of the Scriptures throughout Acts—via quotations, overviews, and allusions—to show the necessity of Christ's death and resurrection (see table 3).

*Table 3. Uses of the Old Testament in Acts to tell of Jesus's suffering and rising*

| Acts | Old Testament Passage(s) | Message |
|---|---|---|
| Acts 3 | Genesis 12:1–3; Exodus 3:6, 15–16; Deuteronomy 18:15–19 | What has occurred in the Christ event is fulfillment of promises to the patriarchs (Acts 3:13, 25). He is the prophet like Moses who would come (Acts 3:22–23). In general, "all the prophets" speak unanimously about this Jesus (Acts 3:18–26; 10:43), including his suffering. |
| Acts 4 | Psalm 118:22 | The rejection but ultimate victory of Jesus is foretold by the psalmist (Acts 4:11). |
| Acts 7 | The patriarchs, the exodus, and the tabernacle are highlighted. | Stephen argues that just as God's people in the Old Testament resisted his plan and spokespersons, so the leaders in Jerusalem have continued the unfaithfulness of God's people in their rejection and crucifixion of Jesus. |
| Acts 8:26–39 | Isaiah 53:7–8 | Philip explains to the Ethiopian eunuch that Jesus was the suffering servant promised by Isaiah (Acts 8:35) and, in light of the phrase "beginning with this Scripture," presumably other passages from the Old Testament. |
| Acts 13:16–39 | Old Testament narrative and Psalms 2:7; 16:10; Isaiah 55:3 | Paul argues to Jews and God-fearers in the synagogue in Antioch Pisidia that Jesus is the fulfillment of the promises of the Old Testament, particularly highlighting verses that argue for the Messiah's resurrection from the dead. |

These passages from the first half of Acts reveal that the Old Testament clearly foretold of Christ's death and resurrection and that this would be central to the preaching of the early church.

In addition to Christ's accomplished work, the Old Testament also foretold the yet-to-be-done work of the church. What is that? What is the church's mission according to the Old Testament? "Repentance for the forgiveness of sins should be proclaimed in his name to all nations, beginning from Jerusalem" (Luke 24:47). In a single summary paragraph, Jesus gives us both his mission and the church's mission. His work was to die and to rise; the church's work is to witness to what Christ has done. Or as Brian Tabb argues, "Thus, at the end of Luke's Gospel, the risen Lord reviews his suffering and resurrection, and also previews the mission to all nations, showing that both of these follow the script of the Scriptures."[3]

How is that witness described? The message that the church will proclaim is "repentance for the forgiveness of sins." The scope of that proclamation is "to all nations, beginning from Jerusalem." The power that will enable the fledgling church to accomplish such a demanding task will be provided "from on high"—that is, by the promised Spirit sent from the Father. It is the second part of Jesus's summary (namely, the church's witness) that comes to the fore in the book of Acts, for as Peter Bolt has argued, "After announcing the third element (the proclamation of forgiveness of sins), *the only one still to be fulfilled*, Jesus declares the disciples his witnesses and promises them ability from on high."[4]

Let us now turn to Acts 1, where Luke begins his sequel in much the same way as he ended his Gospel.

## Acts 1:8: "You Will Receive Power" for Witness

So when they had come together, they asked him, "Lord, will you at this time restore the kingdom to Israel?" He said to them, "It is not for you to know times or seasons that the Father has fixed by his own authority. But you will receive power when the Holy Spirit has come upon you, and you will

---

3. Brian J. Tabb, *After Emmaus: How the Church Fulfills the Mission of Christ* (Wheaton, IL: Crossway, 2021), 22–23.

4. Peter Bolt, "Mission and Witness," in *Witness to the Gospel: The Theology of Acts*, ed. I. Howard Marshall and David Peterson (Grand Rapids, MI: Eerdmans, 1998), 197 (emphasis added).

be my witnesses in Jerusalem and in all Judea and Samaria,
and to the end of the earth." (Acts 1:6–8)

Notice, first, the repetition of (1) the promise of the power of the
Holy Spirit enabling (2) the witness of the church (3) going to the
ends of the earth. Let's look more closely at these three themes as
they develop in Acts.

## POWER WHEN THE HOLY SPIRIT COMES

Jesus tells the disciples to wait in Jerusalem for the Holy Spirit. In
light of Luke 24:49 as a parallel to Acts 1:8, we recall that the promise is for "power from on high." Luke is relying on Isaiah 32 to help
us understand the cataclysmic shift that the Holy Spirit brings. In
Isaiah 32:9–14, we hear of the judgment of God on the infidelity of
his people. Under the just condemnation of God, the people of God
and the land of God waste away. But verses 15–20 tell us that everything changes when "the Spirit is poured upon us from on high" (Isa.
32:15). Thus, we understand Luke 24:49 and Acts 1:8 as pointing to
the last-days restoration, an era marked by righteousness and peace,
which is possible only through the giving of the Spirit. If this is true,
then other prophecies related to the last-days restoration by the Spirit
of God must follow—namely, the ingathering of the nations.

This is Peter's point in Acts 2. At Pentecost, the outpouring of the
Spirit fulfills the Old Testament promise of the last days' empowering
of the Spirit (Joel 2:28–29). The enabling activity of the Spirit is on
all flesh, equipping all of God's people to speak as witnesses of what
God has done. During the celebration of the firstfruits of the harvest,
the Lord of the harvest gifts the church with his Spirit to thrust them
out into the harvest, for "it shall come to pass that everyone who
calls on the name of the LORD shall be saved" (Joel 2:32; see also Acts
2:21). In Acts, following Joel, the power granted by the Spirit has a

missional, evangelistic intent. Men and women will be saved through the church's witness.

As many have noticed, the multilingual witness of the Pentecost church seems to be an undoing of the confusion of Babel (Gen. 11:1–9). At Babel, the lone culture of humanity is divided and scattered abroad into the ethnolinguistic peoples of the earth. At Babel, God comes down to confuse their languages. At Pentecost, Jews who have been scattered throughout the nations are gathered to Jerusalem and hear the gospel in their own languages (Acts 2:6–11). At Pentecost, the Spirit comes down to enable miraculous, multilingual communication.

Pentecost is both an initial ingathering of the Jews from the dispersion and a harvest of other peoples, pointing to what is to come.

## The Witness of the Church

In chapter 5, we considered Isaiah 43 as an example of the reception of the exodus later in the Old Testament. It is good that we did so, for Isaiah 43 undergirds Acts 1:8. It is in Isaiah 43 that we see God calling his people to witness. To what will they witness?

> "I, I am the Lord,
>     and besides me there is no savior.
> I declared and saved and proclaimed,
>      when there was no strange god among you;
>      and *you are my witnesses*," declares the Lord, "and I am
>          God." (vv. 11–12)

God's people—after he has saved them and they have rid themselves of their foreign gods—will be his witnesses. They will witness to who he is ("I am the Lord," the Savior; "I am God") and what he has done ("declared and saved and proclaimed"). Just as in the book of Exodus,

God's person and deeds constitute the message. Said another way, Acts 1:8, in fulfillment of Isaiah 43, declares that God's people will witness to the commencement of the new exodus. God has revealed himself again as the Redeemer. He has rescued a people once more. This rescue, though, is greater and will be everlasting. The disciples "are witnesses of these things" (Luke 24:48).

I have already argued that while *revelation for relationship in creation* is a summary of the mission of God, *witness* is an accurate description of the mission of the church.[5] Let's consider for a moment what is meant by "witness." A witness gives courtroom testimony. This testimony is not like one's personal testimony today, which might be shared with a friend or at church. No, this word is forensic, carrying the sense of an eyewitness. The first Christians were, literally, witnesses of the life, death, resurrection, and ascension of Jesus. Acts records their testimony, their witness, so that we later Christians have access to this irrefutable evidence.

Throughout the rest of the book of Acts, the church witnesses. They bear witness to the life and work of Christ. They provide evidence. They testify to its truth. Roughly two dozen times, Jesus's followers are described as bearing witness or providing testimony. Peter in particular stresses that the disciples were physically present and can verify what Jesus did (Acts 3:15; 5:32; 10:39).

This ability to witness to what Jesus did was a nonnegotiable in selecting a replacement for Judas among the apostles. The new member, according to Peter, must "become with us a witness to his

---

5. For an understanding of how "mission" as the activity of God in sending Jesus for the salvation of the world relates to the "witness" of his people, see Bolt, "Mission and Witness," 191–214. There Bolt argues that "mission" describes God's activity in sending the Son, and "witness" refers exclusively to what the apostles (the eyewitnesses) do. Those who are not eyewitnesses, then, evangelize based on the testimony of the eyewitnesses, the apostles. Acts preserves the eyewitness account, and so we too evangelize by proclaiming the testimony of the apostles. Whether one accepts this separation of the apostles' witness from other believers' evangelism, the point remains that there is an activity of God in mission that is complete, and that the church witnesses to that completed work.

resurrection" (Acts 1:22). Later, Paul recounts his commissioning spoken through Ananias in Damascus, "You will be a witness for him to everyone of what you have seen and heard" (Acts 22:15), and from Jesus himself: "I have appeared to you for this purpose, to appoint you as . . . a witness to the things in which you have seen me and to those in which I will appear to you" (Acts 26:16). And when summarizing his mission, Paul says, "The ministry that I received from the Lord Jesus [is] to testify to the gospel of the grace of God" (Acts 20:24). Acts will end with Paul continuing to testify during his imprisonment in Rome (Acts 28:23).

Elsewhere, the witness of the death and resurrection of Christ by the apostles is put forward as incontrovertible evidence for the gospel and for their own ministries. Peter can appeal to his readers to trust him because he is "a witness of the sufferings of Christ" (1 Pet. 5:1). First John 1:1–3 provides perhaps the most complete list of evidence for the resurrection. John writes,

> That which was from the beginning, which we have heard, which we have seen with our eyes, which we looked upon and have touched with our hands, concerning the word of life—the life was made manifest, and we have seen it, and testify to it and proclaim to you the eternal life, which was with the Father and was made manifest to us—that which we have seen and heard we proclaim also to you, so that you too may have fellowship with us; and indeed our fellowship is with the Father and with his Son Jesus Christ.

John not only claims to be an eyewitness, but he then goes on to testify and proclaim to others what he has seen. To what end? So that, through his witness, men and women might join in the fellowship of the Father, Son, and Spirit.

In short, though we are not eyewitnesses, the church continues the apostolic witness to the Christ event. Our authority is the Scriptures, which include the eyewitness accounts of the apostles and their companions (1 Thess. 1:8–9). Christ, our new Moses, has led a new people out of slavery and back to God. We witness with the aim, then, that a new Israel, comprising people from all nations, will experience the salvation of the Lord (1 Pet. 2:9–10).

## To the End of the Earth

So the church is a witnessing community. And Jesus declares that this witness should reach all nations. Relying again on Isaiah, Acts 1:8 says that our witness will reach the "end of the earth."

*In Jerusalem and all Judea and Samaria.* The witnessing work will start within Israel, but it would be too small for the Lord of all the earth to save only Israel (Isa. 49:6). It always has been. Recall the garden commission to "fill the earth" (Gen. 1:28). Remember the scattering of the peoples at Babel over all the earth and the promise that, through Abraham's offspring, all peoples will be redeemed by the gospel (Gen. 12:1–3; Gal. 3:8). Recollect other promises, like Isaiah 11:9:

> The earth shall be full of the knowledge of the Lord
>> as the waters cover the sea.

The last-days mission is one that will reach to the end of the earth.

Because of this, the early church placed a priority on witnessing where the gospel was not yet proclaimed and the church was not yet established. Therefore, following the progression of Acts 1:8, gospel proclamation begins in Jerusalem, spreads into Judea and Samaria, and then moves out to the ends of the earth.

*Reunification and restoration.* It is often noted that chapters 1–7 of Acts focus on the witness of the gospel in Jerusalem before it begins to move into Judea and Samaria. What is sometimes missed is the reason Christ includes these regions in his charge. We must again look back to the Old Testament, this time Ezekiel 37 and the promises made there concerning the latter days:

> Thus says the Lord GOD: Behold, I will take the people of Israel from the nations among which they have gone, and will gather them from all around, and bring them to their own land. And I will make them one nation in the land, on the mountains of Israel. And one king shall be king over them all, and they shall be no longer two nations, and no longer divided into two kingdoms. (vv. 21–22)

The promise of kingdom restoration in the Old Testament always starts with the redemption of Israel. If that is step 1, then step 2 in that redemption was the promise of a *regathered people and a reunified kingdom* under David (vv. 24–25). As they forsake their sins (v. 24) and again experience the presence of God in their midst (vv. 26–27), only then will the nations come to know the Lord (v. 28). That will be step 3.

In the first 7 chapters of Acts, restoration has come to God's people in the church, who are being regathered under King Jesus in Jerusalem, as we saw at Pentecost. We should, then, expect the reunification of the kingdom to follow. The gospel must bring Judah and Israel back together to fulfill the word spoken by the prophets. And that is why we see the gospel going forth throughout Judea and Samaria in Acts 8–9, culminating in this astounding statement in 9:31: "So the church throughout all Judea and Galilee and Samaria had peace and was being built up. And walking in the fear of the Lord and in the comfort of the Holy Spirit, it multiplied."[6]

This kingdom-reunification thread also helps us make sense of the exchange between Christ and the disciples in Acts 1. Jesus spends forty days with his disciples teaching on the kingdom (v. 3), and the disciples ask him in verse 6, "Lord, will you at this time restore the kingdom to Israel?" I believe Alan Thompson is correct to see Jesus's response not as postponing or ignoring their question but as actually answering it.[7] Thompson argues that Jesus is declaring that "the inauguration of God's kingdom, or the fulfilment of God's saving promises for his people, [is] about to be worked out in the pouring out of the Holy Spirit and the declaration of Jesus' reign in Jerusalem, Israel, and beyond."[8] The Spirit will be poured out soon; therefore, kingdom restoration is at hand. The last days are here; the new exodus has begun and will fill the earth as the church witnesses to the resurrection of Christ.

So, the witness spreads from Jerusalem to Judea and Samaria and continues. In Acts 10 the Holy Spirit descends on the Gentiles, and from that point forward, Luke's attention moves increasingly further afield. Commissioned missionary teams are especially focused on un-gospeled places. Or said another way, the driving vision for the mission of the early church is to secure gospel access to all peoples. Let us consider Romans 15 briefly. Paul describes his philosophy of ministry this way:

> From Jerusalem and all the way around to Illyricum I have fulfilled the ministry of the gospel of Christ; and thus I make

---

6. The conversion of the Ethiopian eunuch in Acts 8 also points to the fulfillment of Zeph. 3:9–13.

7. Alan J. Thompson, *The Acts of the Risen Lord Jesus: Luke's Account of God's Unfolding Plan*, NSBT 27 (Downers Grove, IL: InterVarsity Press, 2011), 103–8.

8. Thompson, *Acts*, 105.

it my ambition to preach the gospel, not where Christ has already been named, lest I build on someone else's foundation, but as it is written,

> "Those who have never been told of him will see,
>     and those who have never heard will understand."

This is the reason why I have so often been hindered from coming to you. But now, since I no longer have any room for work in these regions, and since I have longed for many years to come to you, I hope to see you in passing as I go to Spain, and to be helped on my journey there by you, once I have enjoyed your company for a while. (vv. 19–24)

There are a few important points to notice here. Paul was working in a region from Jerusalem to Illyricum (modern-day Albania). He says that he has had work to do in these regions but no longer does. This begs the question, What has Paul accomplished from Jerusalem to Illyricum? Has every single human become a Christian? No, obviously not. Has everyone heard the gospel? No. Paul's ongoing interactions through visits and letters suggest there is still ministry of some kind to do in these regions.

What has Paul (and what have others who ministered in these regions) accomplished? He has (and they have) planted churches in various cities throughout the provinces in these regions. These churches are now gospel outposts through whom the witness will spread further and further.

In short, these early Christians have obeyed the Great Commission: They have gone, proclaimed the gospel, baptized, taught, and strengthened the believers. They have gathered those believers into worshiping and witnessing communities and appointed leaders for those churches. The churches are then expected to be light and salt in their cities and regions. That is the work that has been completed, and that is the work that Paul no longer has room for in these regions.

So what's next for Paul? Recalling the promises of God in Isaiah 52:15 that the world will hear of the suffering servant and his atoning work, Paul reasons that if "those who have never been told of him will see, and those who have never heard will understand," then someone must go to witness to them. Thus, he desires to go to Spain (Rom. 15:24).

*Beautiful feet.* Perhaps Paul's longing to go to Spain is an appropriate place to finish this chapter. It is a reminder that the letter to the Romans is not only the great theological treatise but also the earliest missionary-support letter. It is an unpacking of the lostness of humanity, Jew and Greek, and the glory of the gospel for all who would believe. But Paul's beautiful gospel theology is then applied to God's mission, for he asks in Romans 10:14–15: "How then will they call on him in whom they have not believed? And how are they to believe in him of whom they have never heard? And how are they to hear without someone preaching? And how are they to preach unless they are sent?"

Of course, the answer to these hypothetical questions is that they cannot. And that is why witnessing feet are considered so "beautiful" (10:15), for saving faith can only come through hearing "the word of Christ" (10:17). Yet again, Isaiah provides the background for our New Testament mission. As we proclaim the gospel, Paul argues, we are participating in the end-of-days restoration of God's global people. It is through the worldwide witness of the church that God will make his name known (Isa. 52:6). This mission is how "all the ends of the earth shall see the salvation of our God" (Isa. 52:10).

The early church joined in the last-days mission, witnessing to the work of Christ throughout the Roman world. This is the mission that Christians around the world engage in today. This is to fulfill all that the prophets have spoken. And indeed, as we move through the rest of the New Testament, we have the deep privilege of seeing that fulfillment.

# 8

# Mission and Consummation

In this chapter, we will survey the Epistles and the Revelation of John to fill out our understanding of the mission of God and the church, and to see their fulfillment. Let's begin with how the Epistles contribute to our understanding of God's mission and the church's mission.

## The Epistles and the Fulfillment of God's Promises

The Epistles are revelation from God. They are inspired missionary documents written by apostles and their associates and sent to newly planted churches comprising Jew and Gentile and their leaders. The teaching of the Epistles on our theme is, in many ways, simply the repetition of what God had done and promised in the Old Testament and how that was beginning to be fulfilled in Christ's life, death, and resurrection and in the newly established church.

Paul, that great missionary apostle, argues that his gospel was "promised beforehand through [God's] prophets in the holy Scriptures, concerning his Son, who was descended from David according to the flesh" (Rom. 1:2–3). The "Law and Prophets" have already testified to this gospel (Rom. 3:21). Peter declares that the grace experienced by the church is the fulfillment of Old Testament prophecies (1 Pet. 1:10). In their utter dependence on the Scriptures, the writers of the New Testament unanimously declare that we are speaking the same good news as the Old Testament.

What is new, however, is the one through whom God's revelation has come. God's Son has spoken to us (Heb. 1:1–3). While the revelation of God's purposes was authoritative and glorious under the old covenant, the revelation that has come in Christ is more excellent (2 Cor. 3:7–11; Heb. 3:1–6). This superiority leads the writer to the Hebrews to wonder how we could ever hope to escape judgment if we "neglect such a great salvation" (2:3).

The Epistles also demonstrate the proclamation of the gospel, including the teachings of Christ, into missional contexts. Some of these letters testify, as we have seen, to the eyewitness accounts of Christ's work recorded in the Gospels (e.g., 1 John 1:1–3). Some unpack various theologies undergirding and embedded in the gospel, such as salvation by faith alone (Phil. 3:9), by grace alone (Eph. 2:8–9), through Christ's blood alone (Heb. 10:4, 10–13), for adoption to sonship (Gal. 4:5), and rescue from hell (2 Thess. 1:5–10, 2 Pet. 2:4–10). Some letters seek to demolish false gospels that set themselves up "against the knowledge of God" (2 Cor. 10:5), including Judaizing (Gal. 2:11–21), proto-Gnosticism (1 John 1:7), idolatrous syncretism (1 Cor. 10:6–22), and licentiousness (1 Cor. 6:12–20). And some seek to instruct the new church in living as a body composed of many nations (Eph. 3–4).

In summary, the Epistles pronounce that the time has come, the mission of God is fulfilled in Christ, and the church is called to witness to this redemption. The Epistles also serve as witnessing documents themselves, communicating the gospel, applying that truth to the life of the church, and refuting any false teachings that arise. They are able to do this because God has spoken in these last days by his Son.

## One People in Communion

But there is something else new in these new covenant documents, something that was a mystery before but now has been revealed in the church age. That mystery is that God's people will include both Jew and Gentile (Eph. 3:1–6). At first glance, this may not seem new, for we recall the many promises that God would bless the nations. So how is the inclusion of the Gentiles a mystery? In short, before the revealing of this mystery, it was assumed that the way the nations would experience God's blessing was through joining themselves to Israel, by becoming Jews. Many of the Old Testament prophecies of the salvation of the nations depicted them streaming to Jerusalem (Zech. 8:22), bringing their treasures to Zion (Hag. 2:7), and even serving the Jews (Isa. 45:14). Paul is teaching, however, that the Gentiles are coheirs, having equal standing before God, without becoming Jews or practicing the Jewish requirements of the law. So, Greg Beale concludes, "Simply put, the mystery comprises how Gentiles become true Israelites in the end-time without taking on the covenantal markers of Israel."[1]

And what sort of share do the nations have in God? Once again, the writers of the Epistles lean on the Old Testament to describe the last-days community. Table 4 reviews the commentary from the Epistles on various Old Testament passages we studied in earlier chapters. The theme of communion between God and his people rises to the fore.

---

1. G. K. Beale and Benjamin Gladd, *Hidden but Now Revealed: A Biblical Theology of Mystery* (Downers Grove, IL: InterVarsity Press, 2014), 164.

*Table 4. Uses of the Old Testament in the Epistles to describe the last-days community*

| Old Testament Passage | Epistle | Comment |
| --- | --- | --- |
| Genesis 1:26–28 | Romans 8:14–17, 29; 1 Corinthians 15:49; Ephesians 1:4–5; Colossians 1:15 | The image of God as sonship is confirmed as we are conformed to Christ, the Son, through the Spirit of adoption, by which we cry, "Abba! Father!" |
| Genesis 2:24 | Ephesians 5:25–32 | Marriage is a parable, pointing to God's aim of communion with humanity in creation. |
| Genesis 12:1–3 | Galatians 3:1–29 | Christ fulfills the promise of salvation to Abraham. Now all who are in Christ are Abraham's offspring. |
| Exodus 19:4–6 | 1 Peter 2:9 | The church is God's treasured possession, priests proclaiming his excellencies to the nations. |

The Gospels declare that God has accomplished his revelatory mission through the serpent-crushing cross of Christ: the true and better David is here, the kingdom has come, the suffering servant has delivered us. Now the Epistles declare that God's relational intention in his mission is being fulfilled in the church. Of course, this begins in the Gospels through Christ's recapitulation of Israel's history and choosing of the twelve, but there is an escalation as the gospel is proclaimed throughout the world and the church is established.

In the four examples above, we see the church defined as sons of God, the bride of Christ, the offspring of Abraham, and God's special possession. These are all relational categories, grounded in the Old Testament, expressing the purpose of God's saving work in Christ. Examples like these can be multiplied for the Pauline and General Epistles.

## In Creation

Where will God commune with his people? The Epistles answer this question in three ways. First, he is already dwelling in his people by his Spirit. They are now, individually and especially corporately, temples of God (1 Cor. 3:16; 6:19).[2] Collectively, they are a living temple, a spiritual house (1 Pet. 2:4–5). Second, God declares that, as an extension of the presence of the Spirit in the believer, his dwelling place is throughout the nations, wherever the church is established. Recall that it is scattered believers in Asia (1 Pet. 1:1) who are called a spiritual house. Paul says to a church in Greece, "You are God's temple" (1 Cor. 3:16), and he tells churches in Rome and Asia Minor that the Spirit of God dwells in them (Rom. 8:14; Gal. 4:6). As we saw in the Great Commission, global mission is a work of temple building in these latter days as disciples are made among all nations.

Finally, the Epistles prepare us for the final, eternal place of communion between God and humanity. We are being prepared for an eschatological city. The writer to the Hebrews argues that this was Abraham's hope—not the land of Israel but a city built by God himself (Heb. 11:8–10). Not just Abraham but all who live by faith look forward to "a better country, that is, a heavenly one" (Heb. 11:13–16). Their hope in this fleeting life is the promise of a "lasting city" (Heb. 13:14).

## Revelation: The Consummation of God's Mission

As we turn to the book of Revelation, we will eventually see this city, built by God, coming down from heaven. But, first, we will see God's mission and the church's mission come to their appointed end.

---

2. While the plural is used in both 1 Corinthians passages, the instruction in 1 Cor. 6 addresses those within the body who engage in sexual immorality.

## REDEMPTION ACCOMPLISHED

In Revelation 5, we are in the midst of one of the great throne-room scenes of John's apocalypse. There we find the "Lion of the tribe of Judah, the Root of David" (titles based on Gen. 49:8–12 and Isa. 11:1–5, 10, respectively) receiving all authority to judge the earth and bring about a new creation (Rev. 5:5). Fulfilling the throne-room scene from Daniel 7[3] (and echoing Ezek. 2), this Son of Man receives the kingdom, the right to rule and reign, because he has been slain as a sacrifice for God's people (Isa. 53:7–12), men and women "from every tribe and language and people and nation" (Rev. 5:9). Thus, Christ's atoning work on the cross is held up as *the reason* he is sufficient or worthy to reign as King (compare Phil. 2:5–11). So, it is also the cross that ultimately sets off the following chain of events in the book.

This image of the slain Lamb certainly recalls the saving work of the exodus. Christ our Passover has died for us (1 Cor. 5:7). His blood has purchased our redemption (Rev. 5:9). Not only that, but he has also made us "a kingdom and priests to our God [who] shall reign on the earth" (Rev. 5:10). This is the language of Exodus (19:6), and it has already been applied to the church (1 Pet. 2:9–10). It is ultimately a fulfillment of Genesis 1:26–28, humanity's first mandate to fill the earth as sons reflecting and glorifying God throughout the creation. The blood of the Lamb brings humanity back into communion with God, into the relationship and role they were meant to have from the beginning.

The "new song" of Revelation 5:9–10 declares that Christ, by his work on the cross, is now able to make all things new. This is a new exodus, a new day dawned, a new people redeemed, and a new heavens and new earth created—all because of the Lamb's sacrifice.

---

3. G. K. Beale, *The Book of Revelation*, NIGTC (Grand Rapids, MI: Eerdmans, 1999), 356.

## RELATIONSHIP RESTORED

Chapter 5 of Revelation has helped us understand the rescuing work of God through the cross as the ultimate fulfillment of the exodus, that great Old Testament salvation image. And Revelation ends by portraying the purpose of this redemption—namely, divine-human communion. The Lamb has conquered. His judgments have been executed (19:1–3). All who stood against him—Satan, the beast, rebellious humanity, and death itself—are thrown into the eternal lake of fire. And the result of this victory is, as we saw in John's Gospel, union between God and man. This union is described once again in terms of a marriage in Revelation 19:6–8:

> Then I heard what seemed to be the voice of a great multitude, like the roar of many waters and like the sound of mighty peals of thunder, crying out,
>
> "Hallelujah!
> For the Lord our God
>     the Almighty reigns.
> Let us rejoice and exult
>     and give him the glory,
> for the marriage of the Lamb has come,
>     and his Bride has made herself ready;
> it was granted her to clothe herself
>     with fine linen, bright and pure."

As one reads these breathtaking verses, perhaps Genesis 2:24 comes to mind. For indeed, it was for this reason that the Son left his Father's side to hold fast to his wife, the church, and to be united with her.

This rich communion is further described in Revelation 21, for the new Jerusalem comes "out of heaven from God, prepared as a bride adorned for her husband" (v. 2). The language seems to suggest that the Father has prepared the bride and is now giving her away in marriage to the Son. The summary of this new relational reality is absolutely astounding: "And I heard a loud voice from the throne saying, 'Behold, the dwelling place of God is with man. He will dwell with them, and they will be his people, and God himself will be with them as their God'" (v. 3). Just as Revelation 5 relied on Exodus for its language of redemption, so here Exodus language of communion is employed. For God is tabernacling with his people, and the covenant formula of Exodus 6:7 is declared over the new couple: he is our God and husband, and we are his people and bride.

This is the point of God's mission. Thus he can declare in Revelation 21, "It is done!" (v. 6). His people are redeemed. The new Jerusalem will be home to God and his Old Testament saints (vv. 12–13) and New Testament church (v. 14), truly one people, one "Bride, the wife of the Lamb" (v. 9). Notice that this will not be a mediated fellowship between God and man. There is no temple, no need for sacrifices, and certainly no veil in the new Jerusalem. No, "its temple is the Lord God the Almighty and the Lamb" (v. 22). So radiant will be the presence of God in the city that there will be "no need of sun or moon to shine on it" (v. 23).

And as we saw in the new song of Revelation 5:9–10, all nations will be there, the peoples of the earth worshiping the Lamb (Rev. 7:9–10) and walking in his light (Rev. 21:24). God keeps his promise to Abraham. All peoples have now been blessed in his offspring, Jesus.

## The New Heavens and the New Earth

John seems to use the name of the city, "the new Jerusalem," as a moniker for God's people, and the new heavens and new earth as the wider renewed creation. As God's first people were placed in a garden, his redeemed people have been placed in a renewed earth in what has been described as a garden city. We do not have much description, but what we have is reminiscent of Eden, for out of the throne of God, out of the midst of the city, runs "the river of the water of life, bright as crystal" (Rev. 22:1). And on "either side of the river, the tree of life" gives fruit and healing to the nations (Rev. 22:2).

Even here, as we celebrate a renewed cosmos, the focus of Scripture is on God's relationship with humanity. For John's emphasis is not so much on the beauty and splendor of majestic mountain ranges, crystal clear skies, or animal life. No, what makes the new heavens and new earth so amazing is this: God's people will see him face-to-face (Rev. 22:4).

This is similar to what we see in Romans 8:19–23, where Paul acknowledges that the cosmos itself is groaning under "bondage to corruption" (v. 21), waiting to be made new. Yet what was the answer for Paul? What was creation waiting for? "The creation waits with eager longing for the revealing of the sons of God" (v. 19). The renewal of the cosmos is a part of God's mission, no doubt, but it will be a new-heavens-and-new-earth reality accomplished by God when Jesus comes for his bride.

## ON MISSION UNTIL HE COMES

That is why the church's mission is primarily one of verbal witness. Between the first and second comings of Christ, we are sent out into the world to plead with people to be reconciled to God. We witness to, testify of, and proclaim the good news that men and women might be saved. We overcome by the blood of the Lamb and the word of our testimony (Rev. 12:11).

But Revelation gives us another word for our missional activity: "invitation." The angel is insistent in Revelation 19:9. "Write this," he tells John: "Blessed are those who are invited to the marriage supper of the Lamb." Blessed indeed! Union with God. Face-to-face with God. Married to the Lamb. That is our great hope.

And that is our great invitation to a lost world. The church, the bride, is making herself ready (Rev. 19:7), but she is also on mission. The Holy Spirit—the missional Spirit poured out at Pentecost, propelling the early church out for witness—and the church are issuing wedding invitations. "The Spirit and the Bride say, 'Come.' And let the one who hears say, 'Come.' And let the one who is thirsty come; let the one who desires take the water of life without price" (Rev. 22:17).

This is a staggering conclusion to the word of God. In these latter days, the church and the third person of the Trinity, in unison, are inviting men and women to come to Jesus, the bridegroom. This is our mission. This we proclaim until he comes.

# For Further Reading

Alexander, T. Desmond. *From Eden to the New Jerusalem: An Introduction to Biblical Theology*. Grand Rapids, MI: Kregel, 2008.

Bauckham, Richard. *Gospel of Glory: Major Themes in Johannine Theology*. Grand Rapids, MI: Baker Academic, 2015.

Bauckham, Richard. "Mission as Hermeneutic for Scriptural Interpretation." In *Reading the Bible Missionally*, edited by Michael W. Goheen, 28–44. Grand Rapids, MI: Eerdmans, 2016.

Bavinck, J. H. *An Introduction to the Science of Mission*. Translated by David H. Freeman. Phillipsburg, NJ: P&R, 1990.

Beale, G. K. *The Book of Revelation*. NIGTC. Grand Rapids, MI: Eerdmans, 1999.

Beale, G. K. "Eden, the Temple, and the Church's Mission in the New Creation." *Journal of the Evangelical Theological Society* 48, no. 1 (March 2005): 5–31.

Beale, G. K. *The Temple and the Church's Mission: A Biblical Theology of the Dwelling Place of God*. NSBT 17. Downers Grove, IL: InterVarsity Press, 2004.

Beale, G. K., and Benjamin Gladd. *Hidden but Now Revealed: A Biblical Theology of Mystery*. Downers Grove, IL: InterVarsity Press, 2014.

Bergen, Robert D. *1, 2 Samuel*. NAC 7. Nashville: Broadman and Holman, 1996.

Blackburn, W. Ross. *The God Who Makes Himself Known: The Missionary Heart of the Book of Exodus*. NSBT 28. Downers Grove, IL: InterVarsity Press, 2012.

Bolt, Peter. "Mission and Witness." In *Witness to the Gospel: The Theology of Acts*, edited by I. Howard Marshall and David Peterson, 191–214. Grand Rapids, MI: Eerdmans, 1998.

Carson, D. A. *The Gospel according to John*. PNTC. Grand Rapids, MI: Eerdmans, 1991.

Carson, D. A. *Matthew*. Rev. ed. EBC. Grand Rapids, MI: Zondervan, 2010.

Clines, David J. A. "The Image of God in Man." *Tyndale Bulletin* 19 (1968): 53–103.

Clines, David J. A. *Theme of the Pentateuch*. Sheffield: Sheffield Academic, 2001.

Dempster, Stephen G. *Dominion and Dynasty: A Biblical Theology of the Hebrew Bible*. NSBT 15. Downers Grove, IL: InterVarsity Press, 2004.

Edwards, Jonathan. *The "Miscellanies," Entry Nos. a–z, aa–zz, 1–500*. Edited by Thomas A. Schafer. New Haven, CT: Yale University Press, 1994.

France, R. T. *The Gospel of Matthew*. NICNT. Grand Rapids, MI: Eerdmans, 2007.

Goheen, Michael W. "A History and Introduction to a Missional Reading of the Bible." In *Reading the Bible Missionally*, edited by Michael W. Goheen, 3–27. Grand Rapids, MI: Eerdmans, 2016.

Goldsworthy, Graeme. *The Goldsworthy Trilogy: Gospel and Kingdom, Gospel and Wisdom, The Gospel in Revelation*. Carlisle, UK: Paternoster, 2000.

Hafemann, Scott. *The God of Promise and the Life of Faith: Understanding the Heart of the Bible*. Wheaton, IL: Crossway, 2001.

Hendriksen, William. *John*. NTC. Grand Rapids, MI: Baker, 1983.

Hoekema, Anthony A. *The Bible and the Future*. Grand Rapids, MI: Eerdmans, 1994.

House, Paul R. *1, 2 Kings*. NAC 8. Nashville: Broadman and Holman, 1995.

Hunsberger, George R. "Mapping the Missional Hermeneutics Conversation." In *Reading the Bible Missionally*, edited by Michael W. Goheen, 45–67. Grand Rapids, MI: Eerdmans, 2016.

Jobes, Karen H. *1 Peter*. BECNT. Grand Rapids, MI: Baker Academic, 2005.

Kaiser, Walter C. *Mission in the Old Testament: Israel as a Light to the Nations*. Grand Rapids, MI: Baker, 2000.

Kidner, Derek. *Psalm 1–72*. TOTC. Downers Grove, IL: InterVarsity Press, 1971.

Kline, Meredith G. *The Treaty of the Great King: The Covenant Structure of Deuteronomy*. Grand Rapids, MI: Eerdmans, 1963.

Köstenberger, Andreas. *A Theology of John's Gospel and Letters: The Word, the Christ, the Son of God*. Grand Rapids, MI: Zondervan, 2009.

Köstenberger, Andreas, and T. Desmond Alexander. *Salvation to the Ends of the Earth: A Biblical Theology of Mission*, 2nd ed. NSBT 53. Downers Grove, IL: InterVarsity Press, 2020.

Ladd, George Eldon. *The Gospel of the Kingdom: Scriptural Studies in the Kingdom of God*. Grand Rapids, MI: Eerdmans, 1990.

McDowell, Catherine. "Human Identity and Purpose Redefined: Gen 1:26–28 and 2:5–25 in Context." *Advances in Ancient, Biblical, and Near Eastern Research* 1, no. 3 (Autumn 2021): 29–44.

McDowell, Catherine. "In the Image of God He Created Them." In *The Image of God in an Image Driven Age: Explorations in Theological Anthropology*, edited by Beth Felker Jones and Timothy W. Barbeau, 29–46. Downers Grove, IL: InterVarsity Press, 2016.

Merrill, Eugene H. *Deuteronomy*. NAC 4. Nashville: Broadman and Holman, 1994.

Rendtorff, Rolf. *The Canonical Hebrew Bible: A Theology of the Old Testament*. Translated by David E. Orton. Leiden: Deo, 2005.

Rendtorff, Rolf. *The Covenant Formula: An Exegetical and Theological Investigation*. Edinburgh: T&T Clark, 1998.

Schreiner, Thomas R. *Galatians*. ZECNT. Grand Rapids, MI: Zondervan, 2010.

Stuhlmacher, Peter. *Biblical Theology of the New Testament*. Translated by Daniel P. Bailey. Grand Rapids, MI: Eerdmans, 2018.

Tabb, Brian J. *After Emmaus: How the Church Fulfills the Mission of Christ*. Wheaton, IL: Crossway, 2021.

Thompson, Alan J. *The Acts of the Risen Lord Jesus: Luke's Account of God's Unfolding Plan*. NSBT 27. Downers Grove, IL: InterVarsity Press, 2011.

Vance, A. B. "The Church as the New Temple in Matthew 16:17–19: A Biblical-Theological Consideration of Jesus' Response to Peter's Confession as Recorded by Matthew." ThM thesis, Gordon-Conwell Theological Seminary, 1992.

Von Rad, Gerhard. *Old Testament Theology: The Theology of Israel's Traditions*. Louisville: Westminster John Knox, 2001.

Wenham, Gordon. *Genesis 1–15*. WBC 1. Waco, TX: Word, 1987.

Wenham, Gordon J. "Sanctuary Symbolism in the Garden of Eden Story." In *Proceedings of the World Congress of Jewish Studies*, 19–25. Jerusalem: World Union of Jewish Studies, 1986.

Witherington, Ben. *Biblical Theology: The Convergence of the Canon*. Cambridge: Cambridge University Press, 2019.

Wright, Christopher J. H. *The Mission of God: Unlocking the Bible's Grand Narrative*. Downers Grove, IL: InterVarsity Press, 2006.

# General Index

Aaron, prefigures Christ the Priest, 69, 71
Aaronic blessing, 64
Aaronic priests, 53
Abimelech, 43
Abraham
  call of, 81
  covenant with, 49
  as father of the faithful, 40
  promises to, 39–42, 106
Acts, use of the Old Testament, 87
Adam and Eve, participation in mission of God, 32
adoption as sons, 28–29, 100
Alexander, T. Desmond, 53
alienation from God, 32
"Ancient of Days," 73
anthropocentrism, 21
apostle
  as "sent one," 3
  as witness the of death and resurrection of Christ, 92
atomistic and moralistic readings of Scripture, 9

Bauckham, Richard, 16, 18–19
Beale, G. K., 31, 101
benevolent rule, 26
Blackburn, W. Ross, 46
blessing, 56

Bolt, Peter, 88, 91n5
Brueggemann, Walter, 46

Cain, 36
Canaan, 43, 82
Carson, D. A., 14n1, 15
cherubim, 30
childbearing, 36
children of God, 36
church
  as bride of Christ, 29–30, 102, 106, 108
  commissioning of, 81
  as last-days community, 102
  as last-days temple, 83
  as living temple, 103
  made for mission in the world, 5
  as offspring of Abraham, 102
  witness of, 12, 90–93, 100, 107–8
Clines, David J. A., 56
communion with God, 16, 19–21, 101
  as aim of mission, 3
  in new Jerusalem, 105–6
  see also revelation for communion in creation
consummation of God's mission, 12, 103–8
cosmocentrism, 21

# Scripture Index

# Short Studies in Biblical Theology Series

For more information, visit **crossway.org/ssbt**.